mindful homes

mindful homes

create healing living spaces with
mindfulness and feng shui

anjie cho

CICO BOOKS
LONDON NEW YORK

Published in 2023 by CICO Books
An imprint of Ryland Peters & Small Ltd

20–21 Jockey's Fields   341 E 116th St
London WC1R 4BW   New York, NY 10029

www.rylandpeters.com

10 9 8 7 6 5 4 3 2 1

A CIP catalog record for this book is available from the Library of Congress and the British Library.

ISBN: 978-1-80065-211-8

Printed in China

Commissioning editor: Kristine Pidkameny
Editor: Slav Todorov
Designer: Geoff Borin
Art director: Sally Powell
Creative director: Leslie Harrington
Head of production: Patricia Harrington
Publishing manager: Penny Craig

FSC
www.fsc.org
MIX
Paper | Supporting responsible forestry
FSC® C008047

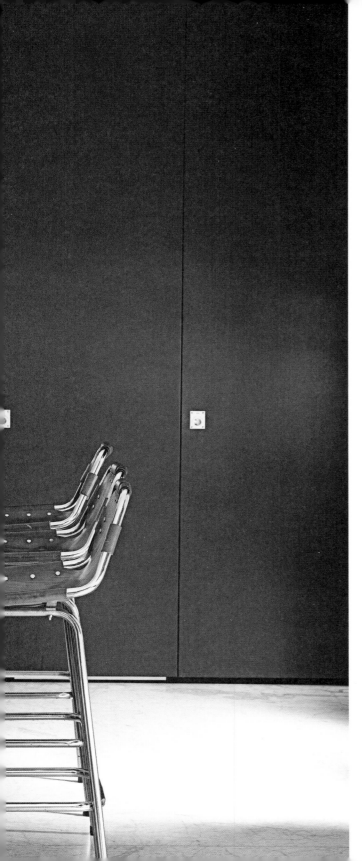

contents

foreword

by **Katherine Metz**, founder of Feng Shui Storyboard, an archive of the teachings of His Holiness Grandmaster Professor Lin Yun

Lean in and listen deeply. Every word, and the spaces between the words, is imbued with the silent whispers of the Masters with whom Anjie has aligned her life and practice.

With impeccable timing in a chaotic world, Anjie nudges us to alter the space around us, to risk the uncommon and allow change to happen naturally. She moves beyond the rules and prescriptions of current feng shui offerings, and her golden threads of compassion and wisdom encourage us to be wholly ourselves.

The guidance is gentle, simple, and easy—a gracious invitation to practice. Even after decades of creating spaces, I was lovingly inspired to sit quietly before an empty bowl. The moment reminded me of my teacher's precious words years ago as he held tight to both my hands, "Your work is to *simply* show up."

Not *just* show up, but *simply* show up. What does that mean? What does that mean today? Working with people to change intimate and personal spaces is not easy. Yet I learned from Professor that change can be simple. I think he would be smiling today at how Anjie has clearly, warmly, and with a quiet mind defined how to be *simply* present. It is in the space of mindfulness.

In thoughtful spaces we graciously and meaningfully meet the light and shadow of ourselves. I met a mother who lost her daughter to a drunk driver and had moved every piece of furniture to face the wall and block the doors and hallways of her home. Together in her space we met the shadow of her grief. I simply made a pot of tea and a glimmer of light returned to her eyes. A beginning.

Mindfulness is Anjie's glimmer of light and gift of grace to see us through such moments, to restore the balance of light and shadow in the places we inhabit. She is our indigo from blue, echoing the depth of the ancient teachings with renewed reverence and relevance, meeting us here and now. I think it wise to secure her wisdom for yourself.

introduction

Humans long and yearn for the brilliance, warmth, and illumination of the sun. We seek and explore spiritual practices like feng shui and meditation because we wish for some kind of change. We think we should "do" something to "fix" ourselves.

My first book, *Holistic Spaces*, was written only a decade after my first introduction to feng shui and meditation. I had studied both and created a firm foundation of clear knowledge. I also understood the principles and could easily instruct others on the concepts. At that time, I felt confident to offer succinct, straightforward tips on what one could "do" to "fix" their feng shui. And now after another eight years, with more experience and gray hair, I am just beginning to see and feel the non-doing and groundless aspects of my practices.

At the heart of this second book is my understanding that each client, teacher, student, each and every person, being, and space is complete and perfect as they are. There is a basic goodness within everything. While writing this book, I was overflowing with so much to share, I had so much to say. So much that it also expressed itself in heavy tears, and a softening and vulnerability I had never yet felt in my life. And I am curious to see what will arise in the years to come.

Please consider and be curious about how to look through and beyond our typical "doing" mindset. This book is not an exhaustive "to do" list, but an invitation to see, feel, taste, touch, and hear your home. Say hello and become friendly with your inner and outer spaces.

feng shui and the mindfulness connection

my story

You probably picked up this book because you intuitively understand that if something shifts in your home it can not only be a reflection but a catalyst for change in your inner spaces.

It started pretty early for me, as an adolescent. I would rearrange my furniture and decorative objects frequently for the sheer joy of it. It was fun for me. As I got older, I heard the phrase, "change your room, change your life." It made complete sense to me that making a physical shift in my built environment would in turn produce some transition in my mood and experience, especially in the little world that was my childhood bedroom.

I always loved creating. I fondly recall a basket weaving class I enjoyed as a young girl. In class, we patiently soaked long rigid reeds of grasses and woods until they softened in the water. Carefully we began to overlap and weave together these different strands until eventually there was a pretty little basket. As an adult I look back at this memory; it offers me so much richness. The different strands are like my cultural heritage from the East, with the influence of growing up as an Asian American in the West. The handsome visual exterior juxtaposed with the useful and practical interior also serves as a symbol of our inner and outer environments. This is a metaphor for my life's work and exploration of feng shui and meditation. My *raison d'être* is clearly about weaving together East and West, inner and outer, into a beautiful and bountiful container to give space to shape our experiences.

As my understanding of feng shui deepened, so did my devotion to exploring Buddhist philosophy and meditation. These two practices seemed to weave together all of the things in the world that brought me joy and enrichment: Space, design, people, beauty, and compassion.

Feng shui became for me a practice of "mindful spaces." Naturally, my definition and understanding of feng shui started to take on a life of its own. For me, feng shui is a mindfulness-based practice, because our environments are connected to and resonate with us. Feng shui is a meditation in action, a dharma* art so to speak.

OPPOSITE: What are the strands of culture and experience that you weave together to create your home? Explore how they can hold beauty, meaning, and even usefulness.

*Dharma is a Sanskrit word that points to the truth of spiritual teaching.

what is the connection between mindfulness and feng shui?

I'm grateful that the universe has asked me to share my life study of feng shui. It's my life's joy, my life's work, and encapsulates my understanding of the world. However, because I have been requested to share and teach on this subject, it has challenged me to contemplate the why. I trusted and knew that these were practices I was magnetized to, but why did it bring me joy? How has the mindful practice of feng shui created harmony and peace for me?

I consider and approach feng shui as a mindfulness practice, but what is the connection between mindfulness and feng shui? And why does it matter? Why am I writing this book and how can it be of benefit to others?

I have seen that feng shui is an extremely helpful healing modality, because it is working on our exterior environments. For most people, it feels much safer and more practical to start to make small external shifts, rather than internal ones. But as we go through the motions of changing all the things in our homes, we begin to make subtle connections to our inner worlds. We can begin to see that our inner lives are inextricably interwoven with our spaces, our communities, and that our joy comes from being in relationship to others.

A good friend of mine, a doctor of East Asian medicine, told me that traditionally Chinese medicine practitioners were encouraged to work first with the more subtle and esoteric practices like feng shui and cosmology before moving on to more directly invasive procedures of herbs and needles. In fact, traditional East Asian medicine encompasses the esoteric methods of face reading, feng shui, divination, qi gong, and tai qi alongside the more practical ones of nutrition, herbs, and acupuncture. This illustrates the holistic view of feng shui that ideally combines yin and yang, inner and outer, visible and invisible, esoteric and practical. However in our modern Western world, we have separated ourselves from the spiritual side.

OPPOSITE: Our spaces reflect and inform our lives. A well placed chair, table, lamp, with even a single bloom can be arranged with intention to invite a moment of serene reflection.

The Chinese words "feng shui" translate to "wind" and "water"—feng is wind and shui is water. This gives us an indication that feng shui works with the two vital elements that all living things on this planet need to thrive. These are clean air and water, or breath and hydration. The ancient practice of feng shui seeks to bring us in harmony with the elements of the natural world. Therefore, feng shui is not just for the home. This philosophy and life view is for any kind of spaces that we create—natural spaces, work spaces, living spaces, energetic spaces whether seen or unseen, material or spiritual spaces. It's how we as humans live in harmony with our environments.

Mindfulness is the ability to focus and place one's attention on something. From mindfulness arises the awareness of the details in our environment. I am so pleased that mindfulness is becoming more of a household term. And it makes sense! Humans are yearning for more focus, ease, and compassion in our ever more overwhelming, rapid, and disengaged technological world. In addition, during the global pandemic so many of us spent tremendous amounts of time at home and indoors than we ever had before. The importance of a supportive, mindful, and healing home became more and more apparent. We can all benefit from becoming aware and mindful of the spaces around us.

It was a huge breakthrough for me when I opened my eyes to this connection between feng shui and mindfulness. In our fast-paced modern lives, we've really lost touch with how to truly connect to our spaces. I don't think we'd be in the precarious state that we are in with our planet if we all saw how interdependent we are. As they say, we are all made of the same stardust. The phenomenal world, our homes, and nature has messages to share with us. Can we slow down to hear what they are saying?

When we cultivate mindful homes, we can begin to see that the destiny of our lives and actions are intrinsically connected to all other living beings. And everything around us—including our walls, objects, furniture, and spaces—are alive.

LEFT AND OPPOSITE:
Bring in ease and warmth for you and your family with plush pillows or accessories that welcome softness.

redefining feng shui

It's important to begin with some words on cultural appreciation. Feng shui is an ancient practice from China. It is not something one can trademark or copyright, nor is it something that one person can take ownership of. I teach what my teachers taught me, and what their teachers taught them, and so this golden chain of wisdom connects you to all the teachers before them. As I've now formally started training feng shui practitioners, I can see how my students repeat my words. I am also a "mini-me" version of my mentors. It's true when they say: Nothing new is under the sun. At the same time, within that there is the understanding that your experience is a unique and precious treasure.

When I guide my students, I remind them to value their own precious life stories. I wish this for my readers as well. Feng shui is the framework with which you can explore your own expertise, interests, and life references. With feng shui, I believe the way in which to apply one's own experience without "cultural appropriation" is to have "cultural appreciation." Rather than looking for a quick fix checklist to memorize or file away, try out feeling, understanding, and integrating. Then you can apply the fundamentals with accuracy, respect, and dignity. Practice your scales, learn the song, then you can improvise. Meanwhile, always embody a beginner's mind.

Feng shui and mindfulness are both practical and esoteric wisdoms that were developed over centuries when humans lived closer to the cycles of this planet that we call home. Most cultures have their own study of geomancy (examining one's relationship to the environment). When I talk about redefining feng shui, it is about offering you the practice from my perspective, as well as updating what I truly believe we need now as humans.

My teachers believed that the student should surpass the teacher. This doesn't mean that the student does "better" than the teacher. As our world evolves and shifts, so do our needs. The energy is always changing. Dharma teachings are so rich and fundamental to our human existence that they have the space to change and adapt. Therefore, the teachings are alive and must shift with time. In the same way, the dharma is timeless, and the student still has the responsibility to present it accurately and respectfully.

ABOVE: I love a spacious dining room table. It's a place where diversity of minds, ideas, and activities congregate.

I'm looking to encourage you, the reader, to step away from the idea of feng shui as a superficial decorative style, or a way to magically manifest cash. It's so much more than just painting your door red. In fact, you don't need to paint your door red and it's actually NOT about painting your door red. Instead, what about investigating the meaning and metaphor of the door? We can explore and begin to understand that doors are portals for energy and transition. When you step through a door, you move from one place to another and can begin to open doors for new beginnings in your life.

Let's move away from this "fast food" mentality. The purpose of feng shui and mindfulness is not a quick fix. We are all inherently good and you have nothing to fix. You truly are perfect as you are. I challenge you to step beyond the idea that if you fix this, everything will be perfect. But instead, how can you approach feng shui with appreciation and dignity? How can you explore this practice and open your eyes to the beauty of experience? And how can you begin to see yourself more clearly interwoven and in relationship to your spaces.

OPPOSITE: Harmoniously curate your living room with seating to invite friendships and conversations.

RIGHT: Shapes, colors, patterns, textures, and materials are all ways in which we can playfully explore the qi (life force energy) in our homes.

how to use this book

You have the gift to design change into your life. You can start by recognizing that our spaces are not solid. They can change, just as our needs and energies are constantly shifting in a dance. Become the designer of your life. When we change our homes, we change our lives.

1. An empty cup

There is a Zen story of a student that long sought to study with a renowned dharma teacher. When they finally met and sat down together for tea, the teacher began to pour the tea into the student's cup until it began to overflow. The student, surprised, exclaimed, "Stop, stop! The cup is spilling over!" The teacher then asked the student how they could receive any teachings if their teacup was already full.

If you offer an empty cup, with a beginner's mind, this book will be helpful to you whether you are a seasoned practitioner or a newbie.

2. Keep it simple

You don't need to know everything. You don't need to do everything. There's no need to get overwhelmed and try to do it all. Listening to what your intuition tells you is the most important thing for you to do.

Like the sun covered on a cloudy day, your wisdom is within you.

3. Use the book as an Oracle

You can read the book from beginning to end, or use it as an oracle (or do both!).

How to use a book as an oracle:
- Take a deep inhale, long exhale
- Touch in with yourself and hold the book to your heart or third eye
- "Randomly" open the book and see what presents itself to you

4. See and feel – trust your experience first

Begin to activate a different way of seeing by "looking" at this book with new eyes.
- Look at the words, but also look at the images
- How do the colors and shape of the words on the page make you feel?
- Are you in the beginning, middle, or end of the book, or the page, or your day? Or your life?
- Have curiosity beyond the words—seek out your experience
- Celebrate and embrace whatever arises

5. Smell the roses

I think this is the most important reminder. It would be a missed opportunity if you thought you could look at a photo of a rose and think that now you have seen a rose. A rose, is a rose, is a rose. But really, please, go out and experience a rose. Smell it, look at it. See the bud open, bloom, and fade away.

Similarly, it would be a shame for you to think that you can learn about feng shui by reading about it in a book. We're so fortunate to live in a time when we have access to all the knowledge we could possibly want, at our fingertips via a smartphone. However, wisdom and experience is not something you can look up on the internet. So, don't just read what I wrote here. Try what I say out for yourself. Explore. Test it. Don't just take my word for it.

What is your experience? Go outside and smell the roses!

the unseen flow of qi

- What is qi?
- Experiencing the qi of yin and yang
- Balancing yin and yang, the inner and outer
- The art of placement: the commanding position
- Feng shui crystal balls

Before we dive in, I want to familiarize you with a basic overview of energy from the feng shui perspective. It's all about the qi! The concepts in this chapter are at the core of feng shui. To truly understand this wisdom, you must start here.

what is qi?

Qi is an unseen life force energy that flows in, through, and around all living things. If you practice yoga, it's similar to prana, the vital breath of life. There is also qi in the spaces that move around you, as well as the chair you are sitting in, and the book you are holding in your hands right now.

In feng shui we always follow the qi, and seek to cultivate and enhance it. East Asian modalities like Chinese medicine, martial arts, and feng shui all look at how the qi flows in and around the meridians or chakras of your physical and energetic bodies of your environment, your home, and your person. These practices also look at where there may be qi that is stuck, blocked, or stagnant.

Feng shui looks not only at the qi in your home and physical spaces, but also your inner and personal qi. Many people understand that feng shui may work with the flow of energy in a space, but sometimes the connection to our personal qi has been forgotten. The home and the body deeply affect and impact each other. In fact, they are interdependent.

OPPOSITE: What does the qi feel and look like in your home? We can use feng shui principles to connect us to the natural world so we can benefit.

what is yin and yang?

You may be familiar with the yin yang symbol, what we call in feng shui the "tai qi." What most people don't know is that the tai qi symbol is not a static, flat, two-dimensional image. It is intended to represent the constant flow of energy, or qi. Qi is an unseen life force energy that is three-dimensional and moving.

    The tai qi symbolizes the dancing interplay between yin and yang. The greater yang is the white teardrop with a tiny dot of black, or lesser yin. The greater yin is the black teardrop shape with the white dot of the lesser yang. Continue by visualizing that the tai qi symbol is getting bigger and smaller, it's three dimensional, while the yin and yang teardrops and dots also begin to expand and shift in relationship to the other. It's always changing.

    While it may seem that yin and yang are expressions of duality, I like to call yin and yang the ultimate non-binary. This concept of yin and yang actually eloquently celebrates the non-duality and paradoxical unity of two opposites. There cannot be yin without yang, and yang without yin. It is a yes/and situation. You can't have the moon without the sun, heaven without earth, darkness without light, an inside without the outside. One cannot exist without the other and can only exist in relationship to the other. Furthermore, within the polarities of yin and yang, there are degrees of expression. For instance, in the winter it's cold in your home, yet it's probably even colder outside. So, in relation to the outside, your warmer home is more yang compared to the exterior. Cold indoor winter temperatures are yin in relationship to a warm home in the early summer.

Lesser Yin

Greater Yang

Greater Yin

Lesser Yang

Here's a short list of the general categories of yin and yang energies. Please keep in mind that a complete list would be infinite.

Yin	Yang
Inner	Outer
Darkness / Black	Brightness / White
Feminine	Masculine
Earth	Heaven
Moon	Sun
Midnight / Nighttime	Noon / Daytime
Winter	Summer
Cold	Hot
Feelings & Thoughts	Action & Expression
Unconscious	Conscious
Interior	Exterior
Cool colors	Warm colors
Hidden	Revealed

In the context of this book, it would be helpful to associate yin with the inner and yang as the outer. The concept of yin and yang comes from Taoism, the philosophy that informs many of the foundational East Asian modalities including feng shui, the I-Ching, traditional Chinese Medicine, and many others. Yin and yang are considered the building blocks of all qi according to East Asian cosmology.

Yin and yang also gave birth to the Taoist ideology of heaven, earth, and humanity. Heaven is yang, and earth is yin. Heaven is symbolized by a circle, like your head, our thoughts, and is connected to our guiding principles. By contrast, earth is square and flat. When you look down at your two feet, the soles are flat on the earth, they make a flat square shape. Earth gives us support and keeps us from floating away to the clouds. In between the heavenly and earthly realms is the way of humanity. Humans have free will and embody the spark of life and qi. In feng shui, the floor is the earth, the ceiling is heaven, and the space in-between is the realm of humanity. Ancient Asian wisdom continually asks the question: how can we connect the way of heaven and the stability of earth? For instance, how do we connect our head with our feet? How do we walk the life we aspire to? Or how do we bring the gifts from the skies down to earth? How do we make it rain to nourish our crops? Again, it's about living in relationship to and connecting yin and yang, the inner and the outer. How can we shift our outer and visible spaces to make improvements to our inner and invisible spaces?

experiencing the qi of yin and yang

One way to begin to understand qi from a deeper perspective is first to acknowledge and then experience. Here are two feng shui exercises that I encourage you to try so that you can begin to feel qi and gain insight from your experience of yin and yang in your home as well as your body.

Yang qi: your home

You can begin to observe the qi that moves in your home by starting with the earth environment around it. What are some of the qualities of yang qi in your home? Take time to review the energetics of the people, the trees, the land, and the neighborhood you live in. All of the qi around you affects your personal qi.

Yang outer qi home daily path:

Let's examine the qi of your home. Set aside a few minutes to do this exercise where you simply walk through your daily path from the moment you wake up until you walk out the door.

Try this just upon waking up in the morning. Get out of bed, go to the bathroom or whatever you do and however you start your day. Literally walk through your typical daily path and take notice of the flow. I like to imagine myself as a river dragon slowly swimming through space along this path.

Contemplate this path. Some things to consider:
- Is it easy to move through your home?
- Are there obstacles, or is the qi smooth? Is there anything in your way?
- Do the doors open easily, can you walk spaciously?
- Do you see something that makes you feel happy or feel dread?
- How does it feel?

OPPOSITE: **In general, white is a beneficial color for your dishes, because it provides a blank canvas to invite colorful meals.**

ABOVE: **A heart-shaped stone is seen as an auspicious gift from nature. If you meet one, touch in and see what message it has for you.**

OPPOSITE: **Painting a door a contrasting color can strengthen your voice and in this case, invite some creativity.**

Yin qi: your physical, emotional, and energetic body

When we talk about your personal qi, it's not just your health, but also the quality of the energy you see in yourself, or what you show to the world. Personal qi can be expressed through your physical features, your outward appearance and actions as well as your words, movements, thoughts, and emotions.

Yin personal qi body scan

Find a comfortable position, and take a moment to relax. Breathe, inhale and exhale. You can close your eyes or gently lower your gaze as we move through a personal qi body scan from your feet to your head.

As you place your attention on the different areas of the body, you'll visualize a color aura radiating around it, bathing that area in color and light. For each body part, gently notice and acknowledge if any physical sensations arise.

Notice the quality of the color. Is it bright or dull? Is the aura large or small? Dense or translucent? Are there any thoughts, feelings, emotions, words, or images that come up? Sometimes nothing will arise. Take note of that as well.

Feet: green aura, connected to new beginnings and growth
Hips: purple aura, connected to your wealth and prosperity
Eyes: red aura, connected to inspiration and visibility
Abdomen: pink aura, connected to love and the mother
Mouth: white aura, connected to communication and joy
Head: gray aura, connected to benefactors and the father
Ears: black aura, connected to career and connection
Hands: dark blue aura, connected to self-cultivation and spirituality

Finally we close the meditation by visualizing our entire body basking in vibrant healing golden sunlight. Then that sunlight extends out and radiates from the center of your heart, touching the hearts of others, and diffuses the healing glow of yellow to all sentient beings. (Each body area and color is associated with the qi of one of the five elements and the feng shui bagua mandala that we'll cover later in this chapter).

You can find an audio and video version of this meditation instruction at: mindfulhomesbook.com.

the art of placement: the commanding position

When you follow the qi, the next step is to see your relationship to energy in space. This is where we can begin to look at how we intentionally place ourselves in a physical place. The "commanding position" is a foundational principle of feng shui. It's what I fondly describe as "where the mafia boss would sit in a restaurant." I've never met a mafia boss; however, I've met plenty of regular people that naturally gravitate toward this placement.

Basically, the commanding position depends first on locating the primary flow of qi into the space, like the main or formal door of a room. In feng shui we call the formal front door of a home the "mouth of qi," because it is where the energy flows into the home. Each room also has its own flow from the primary door to the bedroom, desk, or kitchen area. You want to position yourself so that you can see the door (where the qi comes in) without being directly in line and in front of the door. Typically, that means your back is supported by the wall diagonally across from the door. I've included a diagram to help you visualize it.

The commanding position comes from what we call in feng shui the "four celestial animals," or the less fancy name, "the easy armchair position." The four celestial guardian animals are the black tortoise in the back, the red phoenix in the front, with the white tiger and the green dragon on either side. In this diamond formation, they create the easy armchair layout where the tortoise is the support in the back, like the back of the armchair. We then have the tiger and dragon on either side, like the arm rests, and then the phoenix is the low view in the front. Your back is protected, sides are supported, and you have the widest perspective in front of you.

The four celestial guardian animals

OPPOSITE: **Doors are where the qi enters your spaces. How does your formal entry greet you?**

If we come back to the mafia boss, they would want to sit with a clear view of the door without being directly in line with the door. Their back would be up against the wall, protected. We can also think about where a CEO is typically located in a space. The administrative area would be up in front at the entrance, and the CEO would be all the way in back in the best corner office.

The commanding position can be applied to any location; however, in general it makes the most sense for you to focus on your bed, your desk, and the stove. The relationship to the door varies in other situations, like when you are at someone else's house, or when you are not the CEO of the company. But you (and your partner) are the main person or people sleeping in your bed. You are the one sitting at your desk, and there is typically one person cooking at the stove. You want to place yourself in command when you're sleeping in your bed, working at your desk, and cooking at your stove. These are the three most important placements in your home, because your bedroom is you, your desk is your career or life's purpose, and your stove is your health, wealth, and wellbeing.

Physiologically, when you are not in the commanding position in these particular situations, you experience an elevated level of stress. When your back is facing the door, the primitive limbic portions of the brain activate your flight or fight response. The effect may be very subtle, but just like drops of water, when it's accumulated over time it can wear down a rock.

Metaphorically, I believe there's an obligation to aspire to see things more clearly. I believe there's a seed of desire in each human to be happy. And part of that is to shift our position and turn around, see the world. It's like going through your entire life staring at a brick wall. You don't know any different, but if you simply turned around you would see your life from a different perspective. Then you have the opportunity to experience a 360-degree view.

By rearranging your bed, desk, and stove to face the door, you are making a deliberate and intentional change to see what is around you for a fuller and clearer view of the world.

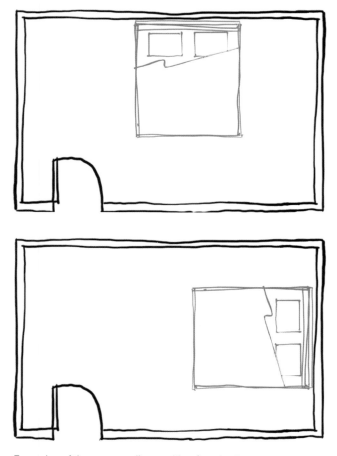

Examples of the commanding position for a bed

Commanding position adjustments

As is often the case, depending on your circumstances it's not always possible to move your bed, desk, or stove into the commanding position. There is a difference between not wanting to move versus not being able to move. I'll leave that up to you to decide. However, if it's really not an option to change your placement in relation to the door, there is a way to manage this. You can set up a mirror so that when you are lying in bed, sitting at your desk, or cooking at your stove, you can see the door in the reflection of the mirror. And if you are directly in line with the door, you can place a feng shui faceted crystal ball halfway between the door and your location.

the feng shui crystal ball

A feng shui crystal ball is a special tool that we use in feng shui to modulate and adjust the flow of qi in a space. It's literally a crystal prism with many facets that refracts light and qi. For instance, if you hold one up to the sunlight, you may see that the crystal receives the light and disperses it to create a rainbow, which is the visible light spectrum. Or you may see an array of small rainbows, which is the sunlight further dispersed and scattered. This is what a feng shui crystal ball does with qi. In feng shui, we liken a crystal ball to the energy of the sun. It's yang, bright, uplifting, and clarifying.

When I refer to a feng shui crystal ball, I am suggesting a specific three-dimensional object. Here are the qualities that you should look for in a feng shui crystal ball:

- A solid sphere
- Manufactured and composed of solid clear crystal (like leaded glass)
- A faceted surface
- Suggested 40mm in diameter
- Has a drilled hole that you can run a thin red ribbon or cord through for hanging
  - Why red? Red is the most auspicious and protective color in feng shui

Two simple ways to use a feng shui crystal ball:

1. To adjust the commanding position

If your bed, desk, or stove is in line with the door, you can hang a crystal ball halfway, or somewhere, between you and the door. You would want to trim the red ribbon so that the sphere is somewhere above or aligned with the top of the door. Be sure that the door does not hit the crystal ball.

The intentional placement of the crystal ball redirects the flow of qi so that it softens the energy coming in through the door. This allows the pointed and direct qi to transform into a porous and dispersed energy, rather than qi that is aimed straight at you like the shaft of an arrow.

2. To uplift the energy of any room

If you have a room or area that needs uplifting, you can use a crystal ball to raise the qi in that place in your home. One way to see if that room needs a qi adjustment can be if you simply feel very tired when inside. If everyone in the home needs an energy boost, this is the perfect adjustment for the center of the entire home.

Simply hang a feng shui crystal ball in the middle of the room, the area, or the center of your entire home, with a clear intention to bring the yang energy of the sun to energize, lift, and shine brightly to support your wishes.

Instructions:

- Clean and clear the object of any residual energies. In this case, I recommend a bath in salt water, and a day in the window to absorb the light of the sun and the moon
- Hang the faceted feng shui crystal ball from the ceiling using a red ribbon
  - Damage-free adhesive hooks are my go to in this situation. Be sure to clean the surfaces of any dust, oils, and debris
  - The length of the ribbon depends on the application, but it can be trimmed to any dimension that equals a multiple of nine: nine inches, nine centimeters, nine feet, and so on
- Humbly set the intention that the crystal ball may fulfill the service that you desire and now embodies your wishes

A note on any feng shui adjustments:

I recommend you bring in something new (or new to you). In general, with adjustments you want to bring in new qi, not more of what you already have. And always choose the highest quality you can afford, with the caveat that you do your best for your circumstance.

Be sure to pay attention to your adjustment objects. Clean and refresh them regularly. When you put anything in your home, especially a feng shui adjustment, it's important to take care of it. If you do neglect a feng shui object, your home will let you know as the dust begins to accumulate. In fact, you may discover that you no longer need it. In this case it can be removed with some ceremony. Thank it and then dispose of it properly.

If an object breaks, that means it has been your spiritual friend and has served its purpose. Thank the object with ceremony, and dispose of it properly. You can reflect upon the mundane aspects of this occurrence as well. In the case of a crystal ball, was the ribbon or hook strong enough? In all cases, if you replace the adjustment tool like the crystal ball, consider using a higher quality string or fastening device, or a higher quality crystal if the crystal itself breaks.

Remember, it's all about the qi. Always follow the qi.

CHAPTER 3

the seed reveals an eight petal lotus blossom

- The nature of the five elements
  - Five element exploration
  - Teachings from the five elements
- The feng shui bagua mandala
  - Teachings from the eight guas
  - How to use the bagua on your home
  - The feng shui crystal bagua mandala

To receive a flower, we must begin with one seed of qi, that holds within it ultimate wisdom and potential. The one splits into two, as yin and yang energies break open to create life. This seed then sprouts to transform into a bud blossoming into the five elements, and then matures into an eight petaled bagua mandala.

This story of the unfolding of life is the story of feng shui. I encourage you to familiarize yourself with a basic overview of feng shui principles we will look at in this chapter because it is the foundation and language that I will continue to use throughout this book. Please refer back to this chapter as much as you can as you read through the rest of the text.

the nature of the five elements

The five elements, also known as the five phases, is a foundational system used in feng shui and across many Asian arts including astrology, Chinese medicine, qi gong, and so on. The five elements are: Earth, Metal, Water, Wood, and Fire. These are universal elemental energies with their own qualities of qi, that are found in nature and are interconnected into a cohesive system that informs and describes our world.

Five element exploration

Your experience of the five elements is more valuable than simply reading a descriptive list of mere words. Therefore, I suggest we start with an exploration into feeling the elements. Your insight and intuition will tell you more about the elements, beyond what can be described with language.

Find your seat, and take a deep inhale, long exhale. Allow your body to relax and imagine that a magic red carpet slowly floats in front of you. You step up onto the red carpet as it starts to zoom away, far away from your home. The magic red carpet begins to slow down and allows you to step off, and you find yourself in a new location.

You find yourself sitting inside an old stone farmhouse in the middle of vast and fertile agricultural land in Tuscany, Italy. You see in front of you a huge, heavy, weathered brown wooden table holding a feast of your favorite foods. You are surrounded by your loved ones. The air is warm and the ground is steady. Then you step back on the red carpet as it begins to fly to your next destination.

OPPOSITE: **Looking at elemental colors only, a primarily metal (white), water (black), and earth (brown) space can still find balance with a light touch of fire (orange) and wood (green).**

You arrive and step into your next location. There is a bustle of excitement and energy that you can feel buzzing all around you. You are standing and looking out the floor to ceiling windows of a penthouse in the middle of New York City. There is shiny metal and glass all around you. You look out the windows, peering down at the fast movement of vehicles and people below. You are enveloped in a flurry of dissonant sounds. Then you step back on the red carpet as it begins to fly to your next destination.

You arrive and step into your next location. The atmosphere begins to darken and you find yourself floating in the middle of a boundless body of water. You feel the cool, damp, dark, and hidden ocean enveloping your body, as you begin to become as shapeless and flowing as the sea. Below you is the stillness of the wisdom of the unknown. And then you gaze up at the vast, mysterious, and endless midnight sky. Then you step back on the red carpet as it begins to fly to your next destination.

You arrive and step into your next location. The first thing you notice is the fresh scent of grass. You see that you are meandering down a straight path within a tall bamboo grove in rural Japan. You hear the wind approaching as the slender tree trunks begin to sway, as if in a dance. The colors around you are a vibrant and verdant green arrayed against the bright blue sky. Then you step back on the red carpet as it begins to fly to your last destination.

You arrive and step into your final location. The air feels dry and hot on your skin. You squint your eyes, as the sun is so bright. You begin to see the red rock formations of the Sedona desert. You can see clearly for miles squinting into the horizon. Then the sun begins to set into an orange and amber glow as the red rocks begin to transform, and you find yourself sitting around a crackling campfire. You feel the warmth of the fire and look deep into the flames that seem to vibrate with the beat of your heart.

Then you step back on the red carpet as it begins to bring you back to where you started. You see yourself sitting just where you are right now reading this book. Wiggle your fingers and toes and gently open your eyes.

If you could pick one of the five places, where would you want to visit right now?

You can find an audio and video version of this guided exploration at: mindfulhomesbook.com.

OPPOSITE: Explore how the five elements appear in your home by looking around you. What do they tell you?

TOP LEFT: Zig zags are Fire; the orchid and green bowl are Wood; the black invites Water; the white blooms and paint are Metal; the flat surface of the tables are Earth.

TOP RIGHT: Bright pink combines white (Metal) with red (Fire); the yellow vase is Earth; the flower embodies Wood, and Water is offered in the vase.

BOTTOM LEFT: The bright yellow wall paint invites Earth to support, nourish, and heal.

BOTTOM RIGHT: Earth element is also present in found rocks. The round shapes invite Metal; the dark colors bring in Water.

First thought, best thought. There's no need to overthink this, just pick one. This can give you insight on what element would be healing and supportive for you right now.

- The Tuscan Farmhouse is the **Earth** element
- A New York City penthouse is the **Metal** element
- Floating in the ocean is the **Water** element
- A Japanese bamboo grove is the **Wood** element
- The Sedona desert and campfire is the **Fire** element

You can explore this visualization and journey through the five elements over and over again. It's enlightening to see how or if your elemental needs change from moment to moment. You can also be curious about when you felt attracted, repelled, or neutral to particular aspects of each location.

Teachings from the five elements

Each of the five elements has their own qualities of qi, and because they are inspired by nature, they embody different aspects such as color, shape, taste, emotion, and more. The list is endless. In feng shui we use the five elements to balance and adjust the energy of our space as well as our personal qi. Here's just a brief overview of the five elements, their meaning, associations to color, shape, movement, material, as well as a few object examples of each.

earth

The earth is where we live, it's the ground beneath our feet. Mother earth is always here for us and will not let us float away into space. She gives us a place to stand and holds us.
- **Meaning**: balance, grounding, nourishment
- **Color**: yellows, browns, earthy tones
- **Shape**: square, flat
- **Movement**: stable, still, firm
- **Material**: stones, earthenware, soil
- **Season**: transition between the seasons
- **Object examples**: flat river stones, yellow flowers, flat earthy square rug

Earth creates metal, like metals ores and minerals that we find within the earth.

OPPOSITE: **Yellow is also connected to the sun. Invite warmth and cheer into your home with a sunny lemon yellow.**

metal

Metal element is strong and sharp like a sword. It can cut through obstacles and help us to refine and let go. And like the sound of a bell, its qi can radiate out vibrations that can alchemize and refine raw metal ores into delicate and extraordinary jewelry.

- **Meaning**: beauty, joy, productivity
- **Color**: whites, off-whites, grays
- **Shape**: round, circular
- **Movement**: contracting, inward
- **Material**: metal
- **Object examples**: metal singing bowls, wind chimes, white fluffy round pillow

Metal creates water, when a piece of metal cools down, beads of water will condense on the surface.

ABOVE: **A bright white room offers clarity and a place for joy.**

OPPOSITE: **Wise black tones can lend elegance and refinement to your home.**

water

Our planet is mostly water with bodies of land in it. We are all connected to each other by the great oceans. There is so much depth, mystery, and wisdom to uncover when we dive in below the surface of things.

- **Meaning**: wisdom, intuition, connections
- **Color**: blacks, charcoals, midnight blues
- **Shape**: wavy, formless, undulating
- **Movement**: fluid, downward
- **Material**: water, mirror, glass
- **Object examples**: a wall mirror, wavy meandering patterns, water fountains

Water creates wood, because when we offer water to the trees and plants, that is when they grow and flourish.

wood

When you step on a blade of grass, it always bounces back. In the right conditions, it grows into a wise tree that observes and moves, grounded in the earth, and expanding toward the heavens.

- **Meaning**: growth, healing, flexibility
- **Color**: blues, greens, teals
- **Shape**: rectangles, columnar, like the trunk of a tree
- **Movement**: expansive, upward
- **Material**: plants, trees
- **Object examples**: living green houseplants, long drapes, tall bookcases

Wood creates fire, a fire feeds on the qi of wood in order to burn and offer light and warmth.

LEFT: Wood colors include blue, teal, and greens which are the bright colors you see with plants, trees, and as you gaze up at the sky.

fire

The glowing embers of a fire can warm our hearts and inspire us. The healing rays of the sun bathes light on us, so that we can be seen for all of our unique gifts.

- **Meaning**: warmth, vitality, and inspiration
- **Color**: reds and fiery oranges
- **Shape**: triangles
- **Movement**: dynamic, expansive
- **Material**: candles, fireplace
- **Object examples**: a red front door, light fixtures, healthy pets

Fire creates earth—as fire subsides, the ashes nourish and transform into the soil of our earth.

ABOVE: **Fiery oranges and reds are Fire element. A little goes a long way.**

In working with these definitions and descriptions of the five elements, please keep in mind that you don't need to have every box checked for it to be an element. Just one aspect signals the presence of the element. In addition, the elements co-exist and flow into one another. Feng shui is a holistic, dynamic, and living system that flows with porous boundaries.

Similarly, all things typically embody all of the five elements. For example, a living green plant is typically thought of as the wood element. However, it can possess all the other elements. The Earth element is present in the soil, the Metal element is in the minerals in the soil (or you can put it in a white pot), the Water element flows within the plant and also when you water the plant, and the Fire element is in the sun that it needs to thrive (or maybe the plant bears red fruit or blooms).

the feng shui bagua mandala

As we turn the wheel again, we will now delve even further into the wisdom of the feng shui bagua mandala and its eight guas.

Bagua is a Chinese word that means "eight symbols" (ba is eight, and gua is symbol). Sometimes I'll refer to the bagua as a feng shui map, because it can be superimposed and "mapped out" over the floor plan of your home. However, I've recently been using the term "mandala" to describe the bagua with more nuance. Mandala is Sanskrit for "circle," and generally describes a geometric pattern with radial balance. I've spent many years studying art forms such as Hindu yantra, Tibetan thangka, and Islamic geometry. Each of these arts explore the universe visually through mandala design. However, you can see mandalas in all of nature: just take a look at a flower. Geometry creates the framework for all of nature, from the structure of salt crystals to the layout of China's Forbidden City.

In the feng shui bagua mandala, there are eight equal areas that radiate from the center. Each gua (or bagua area) has countless attributes like qi, yin and yang, and the five elements. We're just further refining the qi as we get into the bagua areas.

Note: The diagram of the feng shui bagua mandala is just that, a diagram. You may see the bagua depicted as a circle with eight equal pie shapes, as an octagon, or like this in a three-by-three grid. In either configuration, they convey the same information, although the graphic attributes vary.

There are dozens of schools of feng shui. All schools of feng shui are correct, one does not supersede another. As well, all the schools have the same foundations of qi, yin, and yang, the five elements, and the bagua map. What may vary is their applications and interpretations of these core principles.

XUN

Abundance, Prosperity, Wealth

Color: purple

Element: yin wood, the deeply rooted tree

Season: spring

Number: four

Body area: hip

Direction: southeast

LI

Recognition, Fame, Visibility

Color: red

Element: fire, the sun

Season: summer

Number: nine

Body area: eyes

Direction: south

KUN

Relationships, Partners, Self-Love

Color: pink

Element: yin earth, mother earth

Number: two

Body area: abdomen

Direction: southwest

ZHEN

New Beginnings, Family

Color: blues, greens, teals

Element: yang wood, the blade of grass

Season: spring

Number: three

Body area: foot

Direction: east

TAI QI

Health, Overall Well-being, Center

Color: yellow

Element: earth, slow and steady

Number: five

Body area: whole body

Direction: center

DUI

Completion, Children, Joy

Color: white

Element: yin metal, the beautiful jewelry

Season: autumn

Number: seven

Body area: mouth

Direction: west

GEN

Knowledge, Self-Cultivation, Skills

Color: dark blue

Element: yang earth, the wise mountain

Number: eight

Body area: hand

Direction: northeast

KAN

Path in Life, Career, Wisdom

Color: black

Element: water, the moon

Season: winter

Number: one

Body areas: ears

Direction: north

QIAN

Benefactors, Helpful People, Travel

Color: gray

Element: yang metal, the sharp sword

Season: autumn

Number: six

Body area: head

Direction: northwest

ALIGN WITH ENTRANCE WALL OF YOUR SPACE

Teachings from the eight guas

Here's just a brief overview of the feng shui bagua, including each area, the Chinese name, typical "name", associations to color, element, season (if applicable), number, body area, and direction.

Zhen: New Beginnings, Family

The sun rises in the east as each day begins. Like a sprout that pushes out of a seed, springtime offers us the reminder that we can always begin again, with a fresh start. There is creativity in this birth that comes from the joining of yin and yang: mother, father, and child.

Xun: Abundance, Prosperity, Wealth

The tree has grown into a wise all-seeing being, with an abundance of fruit to offer. You are overflowing with generosity because you know that you are a treasure and worthy to stand on this earth.

Tai Qi: Health, Overall Well-being, Center

It's said that the strongest area of a wheel is the center. From the center, the spokes are strengthened to allow the wheel to turn. The tai qi touches, is affected by and influences all the guas. Anything you do here influences your overall being.

Qian: Benefactors, Helpful People, Travel

As humans, we need community and helpful people to thrive. How can we learn to ask for and accept support when we need it? Alternatively, how can we first become helpful to those around us.

Dui: Completion, Children, Joy

The sun sets each day in the direction of the west. We feel the bittersweet poignancy as we reach the autumn of each day, year, and eventually of our lifetime. As each door closes, what is the quality of the gifts, words, and legacy that we want to leave behind?

Gen: Knowledge, Self-Cultivation, Skills

As we ascend up the mountain, we gain skills and endurance. It's a path that is walked alone. When we reach the apex, take the time to sit in stillness and silence, contemplate the journey, and take in the bird's eye view.

Li: Recognition, Fame, Visibility

The red phoenix spontaneously perishes in fire, letting go of what is no longer needed. It is then reborn from its own ashes. We too can bravely open our wings to be proudly seen without shame, and burn away any obstacles in confidence as the sun will rise again.

Kan: Path in Life, Career, Wisdom

In the dark abyss of the ocean, there is much wisdom, intuition, and mystery to be explored. Our life's work is to compassionately connect to and be of benefit to all beings. There is no light without dark.

Kun: Relationships, Partners, Self-Love

Like an empty bowl, there is an invitation to peer inside with curiosity. What do you need that heals and offers ease in your life? And what parts of your life, home, and world have always been there as a silent support as well as witness. What are the ways you can allow yourself to be held, without any fear of falling.

BELOW: This room is primarily Earth, Metal, and Water elements, with a touch of Fire with the candles, and some Wood with the fresh flowers.

how to use the bagua on your home

The feng shui bagua is a mandala that can be overlaid on the floor plan of your entire home (see page 51). Imagine it as a stretchy translucent film that can be extended over a two-dimensional floor plan while maintaining its proportions. In terms of the orientation, I practice and teach from the BTB school of feng shui. BTB is short for Black Tantric Buddhist. BTB is also referred to as the Black Sect. In BTB, we follow the flow of qi, therefore we orient the bagua with the bottom of the grid aligned with the wall that contains the formal front door of the space. That would mean that the door of the home would typically fall into one of the three following guas: Knowledge, Path in Life, or Benefactors.

Not everyone has a straightforward home floor plan, so please don't be dismayed if the bagua doesn't initially work out so easily for you. The bagua is one of the many tools that you can use in feng shui. Also, you need not even use it on your entire home if it's too complicated. Instead, I encourage you to keep it simple. We can use the feng shui bagua in a single room in your home like your bedroom. In later chapters we will explore the bagua applied to your bed and desk. It can also extend to include your entire property or lot, the neighborhood, your town, and beyond.

OPPOSITE: **The flat and rectangular shape of rugs, as well as the brown earthy tones of the wood paneled walls, offer the stability of the Earth element in your home.**

the feng shui crystal bagua mandala

One of the reasons why feng shui and meditation, both ancient eastern practices, are so relevant today is because they are life philosophies, offering loose guidelines, rather than rigid dogmas. Feng shui is a spiritual mindfulness practice that was built with room to shift and evolve. It offers us tools that can accommodate what is required right now—at this moment, at this specific time, place, and in relationship with the energy that is present.

I am immensely thankful that feng shui is so spacious that we can apply the principles based on what is needed at any specific time. While mineral crystals are not traditionally used as feng shui adjustments, I love working with them in my feng shui practice, because they are a skillful example of how to drum in tune with the heartbeat of the world. Crystals can expand our view on how to work with something that is resonating with society right now, and with effectiveness as well as decorum. Plus, everyone is really loving their crystals right now.

Crystals are having a moment for many reasons. Natural mineral crystals, rocks, and semi-precious stones are cherished and treasured gifts from our mother earth. Created within the earth, they're ancient beings that are much wiser and have been around much longer than you or I. They are also magically alluring to hold and gaze upon. A crystal can be small and/or relatively inexpensive. You can also go out and find quartz or other crystals in the forest. I feel that many of us are especially drawn to crystals because it is what humanity needs at this current moment. They can help us to heal by connecting us to the earth, nature, and to the bigger picture. Their tactile quality also keeps us grounded.

We can learn from rocks and crystals. They teach us to slow down, and how to have some ease by allowing gravity to do the work. In the five elements, the Earth element is slow, stable, and offers balance. Crystals bring in this Earth energy that is an invaluable and subtle counterbalance to our modern accelerated lives. The earth is always underneath us, holding us with care.

My favorite crystals, gua by gua

These are three of my favorite crystals for each gua; however, if you know crystals and have your own connection, feel free to explore for yourself. The color is a direct way to start to connect a crystal with the gua connection because the color embodies the essence of the bagua area.

XUN

Abundance, Prosperity, Wealth

Amethyst: connects spiritual and emotional abundance, embodiment of a queen
Citrine: prosperity, self-cleansing
Sugilite: wellness, spiritual love

LI

Recognition, Fame, Visibility

Carnelian: fire, confidence, courage
Cinnabar: protection, wealth, life
Garnet: love, devotion, inspiration

KUN

Relationships, Self-Love

Rose quartz: receptivity, love, partnership, feminine energy
Rough: openness, acceptance
Tumbled: softens sharp edges with ease
Heart-shaped: get to the heart of the matter

ZHEN

New Beginnings, Family

Green quartz: sprouting, healing, growth
Jade: life, luminosity, harmony
Turquoise: creation, birth, connects heaven and earth

TAI QI

Health, Overall Well-being, Center

Tiger's eye: earthy, focus, stillness in the eye of the storm
Jasper: warmth, safety, nourishment
Moss agate: strength, balance, wisdom

DUI

Completion, Children, Joy

Clear quartz: focus, clarification, amplifies
Pyrite: refinement, attainment
Aqua aura quartz: joy, play, open heart

GEN

Knowledge, Self-Cultivation, Skills

Sodalite: skillfulness, truth
Lapis lazuli: direction, spirituality, communication
Fluorite: focus, discernment, enhances study and knowledge

KAN

Path in Life, Career, Wisdom

Black tourmaline: deep wisdom, absorbs confusion and stagnation
Lemurian quartz: taps into ancient insight
Labradorite: intuition, a bridge to the cosmos

QIAN

Benefactors, Helpful People, Travel

Smoky quartz: clarification, focus
Rutilated quartz: heavenly gifts and insight
Herkimer diamond: harmony, wish fulfillment

How to use the feng shui crystal mandala

You can place a stone in the corresponding bagua area of your home, bedroom, or desk to support that part of your life. In the upcoming chapters we will review how to use the bagua in your bedroom and work area. You can absolutely use a crystal to activate the energies in these areas.

Some considerations when using the crystals with a gua

The tendency is to want a crystal in every gua. However, it's better to select one, two, or at most three areas to activate with a crystal. Keep it simple! I recommend you make adjustments to the guas that you want to focus on. The purpose of the feng shui bagua is to see the interconnections of the mandala, not necessarily to create a "perfect" life. As such, not everything needs adjustment. Focus on what you really want instead of watering your qi down.

Some crystal guidelines:

1. Which crystal are you attracted to?

Instead of picking a gua that you need to work on, review which crystal you are attracted to? It's helpful to have a set of crystals that correspond to each gua, a crystal bagua mandala kit. You can use this as an oracle by closing your eyes and selecting a crystal with an intention, question, or clarification in mind.

2. Let the crystal find you.

If possible, let the crystal find you in an energetic sense. This could mean a few things. Perhaps someone has gifted you a crystal. Or, you go to a store (in person if possible) and see which stone attracts you. A fun and interesting exercise is to leave your house with the intention of finding a rock to use for feng shui. Ask the rock to show itself to you. And yes, you can just go out and find an "ordinary" rock. It need not be a fancy, unique, large, rare, or costly purchase.

 The first time I practiced this, I left my home and within ten minutes I saw a rock sitting on a park table. It was very clearly waiting for me. I was delighted to come across this ordinary gray-brown rock that appeared to belong to no one. However, when I picked it up, the bottom side had been cheerfully painted with a teal-blue stripe and bright yellow and green dots on a white background. I was a little bit mortified that I had now just decided to keep a childishly painted object. However, this rock has been a great teacher for me. Mainly it has taught me to remember that not everything needs to be sophisticated and perfect. Instead, it is a reminder to connect with and value my playful inner child.

3. Receive with care

Please be mindful that these gifts from our mother, our planet, are scarce resources. Only take from the earth what is necessary. Do your best to research ethically sourced items. Whenever possible, I do my best to purchase from small businesses owned by women of color. You can also work with crystals that are secondhand. Whether new or secondhand, be sure to energetically clear the crystals (see Chapter 5).

XUN **Amethyst**	LI **Carnelian**	KUN **Rose quartz**

ZHEN **Green quartz**	TAI QI **Moss agate**	DUI **Clear quartz**

GEN **Fluorite**	KAN **Labradorite**	QIAN **Herkimer**

create a mindful space

- What are mindful spaces?
- How to meditate
- Create a meditation space
- Mindful home rituals

what are mindful spaces?

Space is a word that I always come back to. It's fascinating, mysterious, and truthfully something I can never quite put my finger on. On a mundane level, as an architect I design physical spaces for people. As a feng shui practitioner, I manipulate the energetic and invisible in physical spaces. Space can be visible (yang) and invisible (yin).

Although space is empty, there is usefulness in it. For instance, the essential part of a woven basket is the space inside that can hold and contain. My ikebana teacher often reminds me that in the art of Japanese flower practice, we are arranging the space just as much as we are the flowers. I believe this is also true with feng shui and our homes.

In feng shui we also arrange and work with space, because the qi can flow throughout space when we create the circumstances for this to happen. We can curate our experiences and create opportunities to be surprised by what can arise in space. Space is a physical and energetic place in which creativity can flow and emerge, bubbling up like a spring.

This concept of space has been something I've been exploring all my life. While my life's work has to do with examining the yin and yang of spaces, I have also found myself fearing space. With clients, I often get asked, "What about that empty corner or wall? What should I do there?" I have seen this fear show up when trying to fill out the uncomfortable spaces in our lives with the comfort of food, a quiet moment with unnecessary words, or our homes with clutter. Sadly, we've all experienced filling up every empty moment with our devices and social media. We don't know what to do with space. It even shows up in our calendars and our time. We fill up any spacious time slots we have as well. God forbid, what would happen if we were to get bored?

Which leads me to time, a manifestation of space. I am interested in the intersection of time and space, because I believe that time is space. One of the core tenets of Buddhism states that discontent and unhappiness arises from fear of impermanence. As humans we have a fear of death, of dying. Furthermore, in my meditation practice, I am constantly challenged to examine time and space. In a meditation session, one can feel that time takes forever. A minute feels like hours. Or sometimes it's so refreshing and timeless, like a cool shower at the end of a hot, humid summer's day. When we are engaged in the things we love—which for me includes my dharma art practices of mentoring students, flower arranging, ceramics, teaching, or simply spending time with a beloved kindred spirit—time doesn't even exist.

ABOVE: **Living green plants, along with cheerful artwork, uplift the qi for everyone in the home.**

Then as we grow older, we look back at our lives, as well as time itself, and it seems to have just slipped through our fingers.

Someone once told me they knew how to manipulate and stretch time. I was skeptical but also curious. But now I understand. If I'm engaged with what inspires me, that which makes my heart sing, time is eternal. What inspires you? Create some space to explore! The key is not just to look at our outer environments, but to work with the inner through sitting meditation practice.

ABOVE: **Use as many cushions as you need to support your body comfortably in your practice.**

how to meditate

Yes, this is the part of the book where I encourage you to meditate. Of course, it's up to you whether or not you wish to engage with a meditation practice. But I believe it's as essential to our well-being as our breath and hydration. Please, just try it out!

I practice a basic mindfulness awareness practice called *shamatha-vipassana*. In Sanskrit, *shamatha* means "peaceful abiding," and *vipassana* means "insight." I teach meditation in the Shambhala lineage.

Mindfulness-awareness meditation instruction

1. Taking your seat

- Find a comfortable seated position, either on a meditation cushion or a chair
- Connect with the earth, with your bottom if you're on a cushion or the soles of your feet if you're in a chair
- Your legs should be easily crossed on a cushion, or with your feet hip distance apart in a chair. Ideally your knees are lower than your hips
- Lengthen your spine, as if a golden string is pulling up from your root chakra through the crown of your head, connecting heaven and earth
- Relax your shoulders
- Open your chest and heart, strong back
- Your head should be aligned with your spine, not too far forward nor too far back, with a sense of balance and composure
- Your chin is slightly tucked in
- Your eyes are open with a soft gaze downward, about four to six feet (1.2–1.8m) ahead of you. Your eyes are open because you are not trying to close yourself off from your environment
- Soften the jaw

2. Place your attention on the breath

In this meditation practice, you place your attention on your breath. Feel the sensation of your body breathing. This is not any special breath work, just your natural inhale and exhale.

3. Notice that thoughts arise

Inevitably in your practice, you will notice that thoughts arise. The purpose of meditation is not to stop thinking. As the thoughts come up, this is not a problem: just notice them. You can label them as "thinking" and gently place your attention back on the focus of the meditation, which is the sensation of your body breathing. Your natural inhale and exhale.

When you notice you've become lost in thought, gently bring your focus back to the breath. Notice thoughts, label them as thinking, and gently come back to the body breath.

In cultivating a regular meditation practice, it's best to sit for five minutes a day rather than an hour a week. Start with five minutes, and see if you can build it up to 20 minutes or more a day.

I'll be the first to admit that it took me over a decade to cultivate a regular meditation practice. There are a few key experiences that encouraged me to commit to my practice. The first was when I met one of my meditation teachers, he said that he had a student that "kind-of meditated for ten years." I think I turned a little red when I heard that. It was clearly time for me to commit or get on with something else.

Another time was when I heard a friend hurriedly and anxiously dismiss even the possibility of five minutes to meditate because of all of her life obligations. It hit a nerve and my heart hurt. I realized that I too was disallowing myself the time and space that I so desperately needed, that I couldn't even imagine spending five minutes on myself.

Like a typical human being, I often fall out of my daily meditation practice. I just pick up and start again. And sometimes I even enjoy meditation. It was not always fun or pleasant, but I knew that in my heart this was what I needed. When I committed to my meditation practice, things started to change.

You can find an audio and video version of this meditation instruction at: mindfulhomesbook.com.

create a meditation space

We can also use feng shui principles to create a meditation space to support our practice.

Dedicate a place

Find a specific location in your home for your meditation space. This can be a dedicated room, corner of a room, or wherever you can carve out a space for yourself. Ideally you will have a meditation cushion there all the time as a visual and spatial cue that reminds you to practice. Be sure to position yourself in the commanding position, or correct your view with a small mirror. This will support your practice tremendously.

I personally love the combination of a zafu (a small round meditation cushion) on top of a zabuton (large square meditation pad). The circle represents heaven and the square earth. It reminds me to connect to both heaven and earth as a human being in all of my life practices. Some people need two or more cushions depending on your body. If you fare better seated in a chair, you can get a thin chair cushion to serve as your meditation seat. The key is to find your meditation spot. You have permission to have your place on this earth and sit with mother earth supporting and holding you.

The color of the cushions can be chosen based on what you are attracted to, or you can apply Five Element color theory to assist.

Earth element: yellows, browns, and earthy tones for more stability and nourishment
Metal element: whites and grays for clarity and joy
Water element: blacks and midnight blues for wisdom and intuition
Wood element: blues, teals, and greens for growth and healing
Fire element: reds and fiery oranges for vitality and inspiration

A spiritual reminder

It's also helpful to create a dedicated place near your meditation spot for spiritual reminders, like a shrine or altar space. It's not imperative that this is placed adjacent to your meditation area, just a suggestion. You can also have several spiritual reminders around your home. You don't necessarily need to be looking at them all the time; however, they will have more "reminding" potential if you locate them in places of note in your home. I have one in my home's foyer when I transition to and from the outside

BELOW: **Square is yin, earth and round is yang, heaven. What kind of meditation cushion are you attracted to?**

OPPOSITE: **Find a space just for you, that will be your constant support in your meditation practice. There's no right or wrong.**

ABOVE: Shrines can offer a quiet spot for reflection and dedication in your home. You need only offer your love and attention to it.

world; in my meditation area to support my practice; as well as in my office space to remind me that the dharma is infused in all aspects of my life, including my work.

When assembling your main shrine, you could consider what you want it to remind you of. Think of it like a miniature world with thoughtful objects serving as offerings to your practice. You can also include objects that offer feelings of protection, as well as beauty and aspiration.

The Five Elements are a powerful guide in creating your shrine. Here are some ideas to invite the Five Elements, and I recommend you have something from each element to create balance.

Earth element: natural crystals from the earth, ceramic bowls, or the soil of a plant to connect to the earth

Metal element: a metal singing bowl, metal bells, or other metal instrument to cut through confusion

Water element: a small bowl of water that you refresh, or a mirror to invite wisdom

Wood element: a living green plant or fresh flowers for life energy

Fire element: a candle, incense, or other smoke offering to connect with your heart

I frequently move things around my shrines, to stir up the qi. Keep in mind that this doesn't have to be something religious; however it should speak to your spirit.

Some of the revolving favorite objects that I often include are:
• An incense stick and candle to offer light and inspiration
• An open bowl, to receive teachings with an open cup and a beginner's mind
• My ikebana flower scissors as a reminder to let go of what is not required—cut my thoughts—and to wield the sword of fierce compassion
• An image of the Buddha, the embodiment of an enlightened human being as well as a reminder that we all have Buddha nature
• An offering of something I love. For example, giving up a necklace I adore for a period of time to teach me to let go of worldly attachments
• Flowers as a reminder of beauty and impermanence, a reminder to cherish the present moment

mindful home rituals

While I tend to see the world through the lens of interior space, I could also clearly see that mindfulness practices opened up my spatial awareness in ways I had not expected. I was delighted and nourished by my new relationship with space. It was like I could really experience a rose for the first time. Meditation practice can offer us a new understanding of spaces and external phenomena by cultivating awareness.

Awareness practice

I've learned and noticed so much about my home and about myself through this particular awareness practice. It's a great place to start listening and truly seeing your home as a living, breathing being.

- Sit in mindfulness meditation for a few minutes. When you have rested your mind, we will begin the awareness practice. No talking, no note taking, just sit in this practice. You may stay seated or stand for this exercise. It's helpful to have a timer set to ring at five-minute intervals for this
- Spend five minutes looking straight ahead in whatever space you find yourself. You may move your eyes around and observe; however avoid turning your head and keep facing forward. If you feel so inclined, you may move your eyes and shift between heaven—the ceiling, earth—the floor, and the space in between. You may also choose to become aware of all of your five senses: sight, smell, taste, touch, and hearing
- Then rotate your body and make a quarter-turn to your right. Continue with the same practice facing the new direction for another five minutes
- Then rotate your body again and make a quarter-turn to your right. Now you are facing in the opposite direction from where you started. Continue with the same practice facing the new direction for another five minutes
- Then rotate your body again and make a quarter-turn to your right. Now you are almost back to where you started. Continue with the same practice facing the new direction for another five minutes
- Return back to mindfulness meditation for a few minutes. Afterward, take some time to reflect on your experience of your home

You can find an audio and video version of this meditation instruction at: mindfulhomesbook.com.

Go mei wa

In feng shui we acknowledge that everything is alive. You may think your house is inanimate, but in fact our homes are filled and flow with qi. There is a deity of your home, spirit guide, or protective energy that is your home. Our homes are animated with life and breath. They move and grow; we just don't notice because we're speeding around blindly, without awareness or paying any attention. Homes move a lot slower than 21st century humans. But our homes are our silent steady supporters. They are always here for us. It would be a kind gesture to simply greet our homes and even give them a name.

There is a lovely ritual in Japanese tea ceremony, in which there is a conversation between the host and the guest. At this time, the guest may ask the host "Go mei wa" in respect to the tea scoop. This basically means: "What is the poetic name of the tea scoop?"

In my tea studies, "go mei wa" has been an opportunity for me to touch into the present moment. The poetic name often points to awareness of the qi of the environment. For instance, as I write this in late summer, the first days of September in New York City, I might offer a poetic name of "Summer Ripens" or "Glow of the Morning Sky."

When you are in and around your home, what can you notice through your senses, and how does that inspire and resonate with you? What is the quality of the qi that surrounds you right now, at this moment? Simply walk outside or look out the window. What is the weather? What season is it? What am I bringing to the present moment? And what does my home bring me? Look around. Listen to the sounds. What is the quality of the air on your skin, and what does the air taste like? Take a deep breath through your nose and take in the smells. And what does this invoke in me, or what is my personal experience of the now? This is the way that we begin to find messages from the phenomenal world. Look at the yin and yang, inner and outer.

There's much that we can learn from naming a tea scoop. Qi flows all around us, especially in the most ordinary objects and spaces. By greeting and naming our homes, we acknowledge the deity of our home. Our home is a living and breathing spiritual being that silently supports and nurtures us.

Greet your home with gratitude and recognition regularly by humbly offering a poetic name. Let the name change from moment to moment, day to day, month to month. See this as an opportunity to connect with your home as well as the environment around you.

OPPOSITE: **Look out your window today. What is the weather like, and what is she telling you?**

unscheduled day at home

When I was a kid, I can remember how much fun it was to have the power go out, or a snow day. Actually, I grew up in Los Angeles and we didn't have snow days—we had smog alert days! And on some rare occasion, a rainy day. There was excitement, spontaneity, and fun that went along with these disruptions to the regularly scheduled programming of life. An upside-down sort of day.

If the power went out, we would all be fired up to break out the candles, and start making shadow puppets on the wall. We could see our homes in a different light, literally. I remember creating my own extremely interesting "upside-down" world by sitting on the sofa with my legs resting on the wall and my head dangling over the seat towards the floor. The world was upside-down. And it was play!

As adults, many of us have forgotten how to enjoy these unscheduled moments. Everything needs to be right-side up, or we get dizzy and nauseous. If the power went out, how would we get anything done without our computers and the internet?

This is an invitation to schedule a simple unscheduled day at home. Ideally, I'd recommend doing this ritual at least twice a month, but you do the best you can. This is like a mini meditation retreat for me. Give yourself permission to just do whatever you want.

Recommended guidelines for your unscheduled day

- Do it completely unplugged from the internet. Turn off your phone, computer, and other devices. You can even try turning the lights out
- If you can, see if you can also spend this day in silence. If you must communicate, you can write a short pithy note on a piece of paper (no computer!) If you want to expand on this, you can also avoid reading
- Prepare as you need to so that you can have this day just for you. Let your loved ones or work know in advance. And put it on your calendar—literally schedule it
- Any day can work but, if you can, try to coordinate it on or around the phases of the moon
- The new moon qi is about starting something new and growing, like planting seeds, the springtime, wood element, and the New Beginnings (Zhen) bagua area

ABOVE: **What was your favorite rainy day activity as a child? How can you invite play into your home?**

• The full moon is helpful for energy to complete and let go, like harvesting and receiving recognition, the fall, Metal element, and the Completion (Dui) bagua area

Rituals are how humans create change in their lives. We can begin to look at our homes differently by creating holistic sacred spaces with intention. I hope that you can begin to connect with your home through these mindfulness rituals.

simplify and make space

noticing and removing obstacles in your home

A vast feng shui door opened for me when I began to see the connection between the spaces and objects in our home, and how they correspond to obstacles in our lives. These obstacles are part of our path and offer us many rich messages. Literally and metaphorically, we can begin to see how we create physical, emotional, mental, and energetic blocks that often directly correspond to challenges in our lives. It is through mindfulness that we can become more aware, notice, and remove these obstacles.

To clarify, when I talk about simplifying with mindfulness, I'm not referring to clutter specifically. We can have many obstacles that are not "clutter." I've visited many homes as a feng shui expert and as an architect. It's so common that people are unnecessarily concerned and embarrassed by what they perceive is clutter. We can be so critical of ourselves when there is no need to feel any shame. I'm not encouraging hoarding, but nor am I promoting an ascetic, minimalist lifestyle. I am not talking about either polar opposites; rather, everything is included. My life changed immensely when I began to see that every part of me, including the ugly parts, was acceptable and included.

When a home is lived in and alive, it pulses with qi. Qi has life. We say in feng shui, when there is an empty home, completely devoid of belongings, it's yin, or dead. It might as well be a cold, lifeless hotel room for strangers.

People think that feng shui equals decluttering. However, when feng shui was developed in ancient China there was no such thing as clutter. Only in the past few decades have human beings lived in such a consumer-focused society. We have way too many things. I liken it to how as a species, humans are adjusting to new foods, technologies, and overall lifestyles that we have not yet evolved to completely harness. If you do have clutter, accept it with gentleness. The first step is to not be ashamed of yourself.

OPPOSITE: **Simplifying your home includes having enough storage space for your belongings. It's okay to make room for the things that you need. Doors on cabinets and cupboards tremendously help to create calm qi and less visual clutter.**

letting go practice

In life, in our homes, and within our hearts, it can be so hard to let go of things with which we have surrounded ourselves. This can be people, things, or places. And this seems to be the case regardless of whether they are helpful and beneficial, or if they hurt us or hold us back. It's perfectly human to try to solidify, become fixated, and seek stability.

Making space is not about letting go of the things we love; rather it's a practice of allowing our hearts to acknowledge impermanence and attachment. When you give, you receive. When you receive, you give. And if we take it a step further, there is a Zen adage "there is no giver, there is no receiver." I found this Buddhist awareness practice incredibly subtle yet powerful in exploring how to let go.

Here are the steps:

- Pick up any personal object nearby
- Hold it in one hand, feel the weight of it, and be curious about it
- Now allow the hand to offer it to your other hand
- Notice anything that comes up when you shift the object to the other hand
- Spend time moving the object back and forth between hands

If you'd like to take this practice even further, see if there is a slightly meaningful object in your home that you can give away. When I took my bodhisattva vow, I was asked to give away a precious object as a gift to the teacher. Essentially, a bodhisattva is a compassionate human being that has vowed to offer their assistance toward the enlightenment of all sentient beings. I found the vow, and the gift giving, quite meaningful and encourage you to try out and examine this process. See what comes up for you personally. These very simple practices can begin to open up new pathways and allow a safe space to give and receive.

See how you can begin to let go.

OPPOSITE: **Even your ordinary bric-a-brac can bring space for play, joy, and contemplation.**

make space for new qi

Even if you consider yourself a minimalist, it is helpful to shift continually and realign the energy of your home. When we allow energy to pile up and dust to accumulate, it's an indication that there's qi that needs some movement.

When it comes to clutter (and dust), I take a gentle and compassionate approach. For instance, when I am asked how to stop the dust (and clutter), I might smile and shrug. Both clutter and dust just naturally gather in our homes. We can be thankful to them for giving us the reminder to shake up the qi to make space for something new and show us what we have been neglecting.

Simplify with the bagua

The feng shui bagua can help us to interpret these love notes from our home. You can use the feng shui bagua as a tool to see what you might need to simplify in your life. When you overlay the bagua onto your home, or a room, take note of areas that are noticeably cluttered, congested, and/or dusty. You can also reflect on your daily home path and any physical obstacles you may have in your home (from Chapter 2 "Yang Outer Qi Home daily path"). Here's a gua by gua guide to begin a conversation with yourself about how these stagnant areas can offer insight.

Zhen: New Beginnings, Family

You may be stuck and unable to start something new or incorporate new ways of thinking (remember the beginner's mind). Or on the other hand, you may always have so many new ideas and so many balls in the air that none of them get completed.

Xun: Abundance, Prosperity, Wealth

Do you feel as if you are being weighed down with feelings of low self-worth? You may also feel overwhelmed and completely under an avalanche in terms of your finances and/or feel that you never have enough.

Tai Qi: Health, Overall Well-being, Center

Are there blocks and challenges that are affecting aspects of your life? Is there something to examine in terms of your overall health and well-being?

Qian: Benefactors, Helpful People, Travel

Is there difficulty in asking for help or finding support? Or do you offer way too much unsolicited feedback? Explore how you can be a benefactor to other people.

Dui: Completion, Children, Joy

Check in to see if you are inundated with an abundance of projects that need completion. What is your level of joy, and is your voice being heard?

Gen: Knowledge, Self-Cultivation, Skills

Are there places in your spiritual life where you're always window shopping, always climbing and not really arriving? See where you can dig deep and listen to the ancient wisdom of the mountain.

Li: Recognition, Fame, Visibility

Is there still inspiration in your life, or has some fire been snuffed out? Where can you start to bring in vitality and allow your light to be seen?

Kan: Path in Life, Career, Wisdom

Do you feel there is a disconnect between your day-to-day routine and your life path? Is there a part of you that you've buried and hidden? What fears can be examined?

Kun: Relationships, Partners, Self-Love

There may be parts of your heart that you've covered up. How can you gently start to open up and be more vulnerable?

ABOVE: **Find joy in peering inside long-lost drawers to see what parts of yourself you may have forgotten.**

Nine things a day for 27 days

While you internally explore the connections to the feng shui bagua, it's helpful to work in tandem with the physical space. If you find there's clutter, try moving out nine things a day for 27 days. And if you miss a day, unfortunately you have to start all over again with your 27-day cycle.

Too many plants?

These days, many people (myself included) are really loving their house plants. They are a wonderful and easy way to invite the wood element, which is about generosity, kindness, and flexibility. Plants also bring nature into our homes. But, I've also seen a trend of plant overwhelm! This can also be a form of clutter in our homes. Some things to consider if you are feeling inundated with plants:

- Are they outgrowing their pots, unable to flourish?
- Is there dust accumulating on the leaves?
- Is it challenging to care for your sick plants?
- Are you spending too much time taking care of your plants?
- Do you simply have way too many plants?

Consider how you can cultivate kindness and generosity toward yourself by allowing flexibility to let go of some of your plants. If you have ever had a fruit tree in your backyard, you would know it bears much more than any single family needs. This is the definition of abundance. How can you embrace your abundance and begin to give away what you have too much of?

Keep it simple. Do one thing at a time. While you work through simplifying your home start with one space. Just one area.

Engage the alchemy of metal

There is power to explore when engaging with the element of Metal. Imagine a single sharp blade cutting away old growth to allow new shoots to flourish. In my flower practice, the most difficult part is deciding to clip off a beautiful bloom. It's so pretty! I don't want to let it go. What do I do if I want it back? I can't glue the leaf back on! But there is a clarity and joy that comes from allowing simplicity to shine.

ABOVE: **Nature is so calming because it is self sufficient and doesn't ask anything of you. Take time to bring some of this ease into your home by simplifying.**

what is space clearing?

What is space clearing and why is it helpful? When we work with feng shui, we are balancing yang with yin, the visible with the invisible. When we clear the space in our homes, we are working with the qi that we cannot see to transmute it. Transmute implies that we are shifting and changing the qi rather than eliminating it. We can even think of a clearing as a way to bless and imbue our home with new intention.

Right now, as I write this book, it's raining in New York City. And so, the natural world reminds me that the rain itself is a space-clearing and blessing for all life on this earth. When it rains, we feel hydrated, nourished, and refreshed. It smells so good! It's truly a human delight, enjoyable and healing. It's not simply washing away; instead it's revealing and creating new qi.

space blessing rituals

Humans thrive on and crave ritual because it speaks to the primitive parts of our brain. These space-clearing and blessing rituals are celebratory ceremonies that can mark transitions in our lives.

Some of the best times to clear and bless a space are when you are crossing a threshold. For instance, it can occur once a year, or we can celebrate each morning when the sun rises to start a new day. In general, you may want to offer your home a space-clearing and blessing when there is a change or you'd like to make a change.

• When you feel stuck
• After decluttering
• After you've had many visitors into your space
• On ceremonial and celebratory holidays such as:
    • birthdays, the equinox or solstice, western and lunar new years
• Moving into a new space or leaving one
• When saying goodbye or hello

These are currently my favorite space-clearing rituals which have been inspired by all of my mentors and teachers of many schools of thought, including feng shui, Buddhist, shamanic, and kundalini yoga teachings.

Smoke offerings with botanicals

When you burn a botanical, the smoke rises up to the heavens. Smoke has long been a way for us to connect to the realm of the deities. We gather something from our earth, offer it to the fire, and then it transforms into smoke and ash.

When gathering your botanicals, it's essential to ask permission and receive consent. This includes purchasing incense or a botanical bundle, and taking a moment to sit with the offering. In feng shui, dried orange or tangerine peels are a particularly powerful botanical to burn. The contents of our kitchen cabinets also contain magically marvelous smoke-offering herbs such as bay leaf and cinnamon. Are there botanicals you can research that have meaning, or are native to your own cultural heritage? I also invite you to explore what is native to your current location: what is growing outside your home right now? What can you find if you walk outside?

Smoke offering ritual, connecting heaven and earth

- Begin with an inhale, and a long exhale
- Start at the front door of your space, and light your botanical with care
- Circumambulate the home in a clockwise direction. You can follow the wall on your left
- While circumambulating, you may choose to add sound, such as mantras or bells
- Visualize that the qi of the space is being transmuted into bright white sunlight
- Close the offering with a wish when you return to the front door

Note: I recommend that you carry a small candle with you, like a tea light on a plate, to easily re-light your botanicals as required.

Make your heart sing

Make your home sing by allowing your heart to be heard. Your own voice is the most healing instrument that you can harness. You don't need to go out and buy anything, it's all within you. Invoke your own sound current out loud to clear and bless your home.

Take some time to consider if there's a particular song or mantra that would be appropriate. I almost always chant "Om Ma Ni Pad Me Hum," which is a Buddhist Sanskrit mantra that means "the jewel is in the lotus."

Heal your home and heart with sound

- Begin with an inhale, and a long exhale
- Start at the front door of your space and start singing out loud
  Make sure you can hear your own voice
- Place your hands over the center of your heart, left hand on top of the right, palms facing toward you
- Visualize your voice reaching all parts of your home, and that the qi of the space is being transmuted into bright rainbow light
- Continue to sing as you circumambulate the home in a clockwise direction. You can follow the wall on your left
- Close your heart offering with a wish when you return to the front door

ABOVE: **Smoke blessings allow us opportunities to let go and transform. Offer what you don't need to the fire.**

Blessing of objects

You can also use smoke blessing rituals with objects. This is helpful for when you bring in a secondhand item, or any new item, especially if it's used for feng shui or a ritual function.

- Begin with an inhale, and a long exhale
- Light your botanical, using a firesafe bowl and candle
- With deliberate care and generosity, gently pass the object through the smoke
- If it's a large object, you may walk around it while holding the botanical as you would for the space blessing ritual
- Visualize that the qi of the object is being transmuted into bright white sunlight
- Offer an intention or wish for your object
- Close by gently putting out the candle with gratitude

Where do things come from? Ethically obtaining objects

Where do our belongings come from? Qi flows within and around our walls, objects, and spaces. Similarly, qi is also imprinted and memorized within the structure of the same walls, objects, and spaces. Therefore, we are surrounded by energies that we may not be aware of. For instance, there is residual "predecessor qi" in our home from recent visitors, secondhand items, former residents, and the original inhabitants of the land that your home sits on. Even the small items we bring home that are "new" may retain some energy from the different hands they have passed through. This is just one of the reasons why it's meaningful to be curious about where things come from. And where you come from.

Please be interested in where things come from, whether that be something old or new, animate or inanimate. There is a living life force within everything. Similarly, your qi also affects and touches all other beings. What would this world be like if we all had curiosity and open hearts toward each other?

OPPOSITE: **Making a cup of tea can offer us many blessings to soothe our hearts. It's an opportunity to pause, reflect, and create art in our everyday moments.**

meet your heart: the bedroom

- Your bedroom is a symbol for you
- Activate the bagua mandala of your bed
- Ritual: Awaken the deity of your bed
- Feng shui shifts for your bedroom
  - Feng shui tips
  - Five element color guide
  - Activate the tai qi of your bedroom

your bedroom is a symbol for you

Sometimes the easiest thing to do is to ignore your own needs and attend to others. If this sounds like you, I can also guess that you may be the type to spend your time and energy on the formal areas of the home rather than your own bedroom. However, in feng shui, your bedroom is a symbol of you. It's a safe and private place to meet and connect with your own tender and vulnerable heart.

Your bedroom is your most sacred space because it is where you spend a tremendous amount of your time. Your bedroom is just for you (and a partner, if you have one). It's where you go to rejuvenate, rest, and dream. It's also there when you're sick, need support, and where you can heal.

If you are a newbie or DIYer, always start with the bedroom. It is the most important place in the home. Your bedroom's feng shui is the closest space to you, and also the most impactful qi-wise on your whole being. You have permission to put yourself first and look at your most hidden and secret places that you don't have to share with others.

OPPOSITE: **A vase of fresh eucalyptus leaves in the bedroom invites healing, rejuvenation, and the Wood element.**

XUN

Abundance, Prosperity, Wealth

Seal 108 coins of your choice (for instance 108 American quarters or 108 one-euro coins) in a purple envelope with the wish that you recognize your true value.

LI

Recognition, Fame, Visibility

Write a list of nine wishes for inspiration, life energy, and vitality. Place it inside a red envelope.

KUN

Relationships, Partners, Self-Love

Gather a pair of heart shaped rose quartz pieces together here to symbolize softening love for yourself and for others.

ZHEN

New Begininngs, Family

Place a seed (for instance an acorn) in a blue or green envelope to encourage growth from latent potential toward an expansive great oak tree.

TAI QI

Health, Overall Well-being, Center

Place nine grains of rice in a yellow or gold envelope to nourish your health and overall well-being.

DUI

Completion, Children, Joy

Place a small bell, cymbal, chime or other metal musical instrument here that makes a pleasant sound, to inspire you to cut through challenges to communicate and complete tasks with grace.

GEN

Knowledge, Self-Cultivation, Skills

Go out into nature and find a rock or stone that calls to you. Activate Gen to invite wisdom as ancient as the mountains into your heart.

KAN

Path in Life, Career, Wisdom

Place a three-inch round flat mirror in a well padded red pouch, so that you may know the steps to take on your true path in life.

QIAN

Benefactors, Helpful People, Travel

Using a nine-inch long gray or silver ribbon, create a circle by connecting the two loose ends. Place this in a gray or silver envelope with the intention to call in support from the heavens.

activate the bagua mandala of your bed

Most people don't know that the feng shui bagua can be overlaid and activated on your bed. On the practical side, this keeps things simple and straightforward, because your bed is rectangular. Simple and direct is quite effective. Starting with your bed's bagua, it's a powerfully energetic way to start to shift your qi. Take a moment to consider how much time you spend in bed; typically it's around a third of your life. And when you are in bed, you are sleeping in an unconscious "yin" state, and very open and susceptible to the energies around you.

The bagua layout on your bed

The bottom of the bagua map is aligned with the foot of the bed. If you stand centered at the foot of your bed, facing the headboard, you're right in front of Kan position: Path in Life, Career, Wisdom. The center of the headboard would be Li: Recognition, Fame, Visibility. See diagram opposite.

On the diagram, I've enumerated some of my favorite ways to work with each gua using the bagua layout of your bed. In each case, you can place the suggested item or object either on the floor under your bed, fastened to the bottom of your bed, or underneath your mattress. However, be careful to protect it so that it doesn't break, get jostled, or regularly disturbed. And, please choose only one area to work on at a time! I recommend you work with one gua for at least 27 days before moving on to another area. You may keep the adjustment in the position for at least 27 days or until the issue is no longer of concern.

Ritual: Awaken the deity of your bed

This is a ritual to awaken the deity of your bed to support and connect you to your home. You can practice this while actually lying on your bed, but you can also visualize this anywhere. Visualization is a mighty tool and can be equally (or in some cases more) effective.

- Inhale, and exhale completely. Allow your qi to intermingle with the space around you
- Gently close your eyes and visualize yourself lying at the center of your bed
- Allow your body to be held. Release any tension and allow your bed to hold and support you as she does each night, making space for your rest and rejuvenation
- In your heart center, you see a white ball of light. It shines bright with the energy of the sun and the moon
- Then from your heart center, this light of the sun and the moon begins to fill your whole heart offering rest, rejuvenation, and healing
- From your heart center, radiating to fill your heart, this light of the sun and the moon begins to fill your entire torso offering rest, rejuvenation, and healing
- Then from your heart center, radiating out to your whole heart, and then radiating out to fill your entire torso, this light of the sun and the moon begins to radiate to include your entire bed offering rest, rejuvenation, and healing
- Place your attention back into your heart center. The light focuses and shines bright there with the energy of the sun and the moon
- Allow this light to move gently from your heart to the center of your bed
- Offer this light as a gift to the deity of your bed, with humble gratitude
- Your bed receives the gift, and mirrors your gratitude
- To close, together, you and the deity of your bed radiate this light of the sun and the moon. And together you offer this light to be shared with compassion with all sentient beings

You can find an audio and video version of this meditation instruction at: mindfulhomesbook.com.

OPPOSITE: **A strong wall behind your bed offers the stability, protection, and support of a mountain that always has your back.**

feng shui shifts for your bedroom

Here are some important feng shui aspects to bear in mind when it comes to your bedroom's overall feng shui.

Commanding position of the bed

The bed is one of the most important places in your home that you will want to prioritize when it comes to the commanding position. For the bed placement, to arrange yourself in command means that when you're lying there, you should be able to see the door without being directly in line with it. You want to avoid your feet pointing straight out the door. Sometimes the easiest way to achieve the commanding position is to have the bed placed in a diagonal from the door. If it's not possible to rearrange your bed location, you can use a mirror to correct your view, so that when you're lying in bed you can see the door clearly. For a bedroom, a freestanding full-length mirror on a stand works perfectly. If any part of the bed is directly aligned with the door, you might also want to hang a feng shui crystal ball from the ceiling somewhere between the bed and the door. See Chapter 2 for more on the commanding position and on the placing of the crystal ball.

When your bed is out of command, your restfulness and sleep can be affected, especially if you have preexisting sleep issues. If your bed is not in command, that underlying level of stress is especially significant, because you are more open and in a passive state. The bedroom represents the most interior and most private parts of your life and home. It's so important that you are able to see what is coming to you in this very special place. We benefit from feeling safe, protected, and supported while we sleep. We need time and space to open our dreams and hearts to the innermost vulnerable parts of us. If you don't feel secure in your own bed, where can you feel safe? This feeling of insecurity really wears down all parts of you. The commanding position is a tool to help you create a sanctuary where you can retire and be unguarded, open, cared for, and protected.

TOP LEFT: **Purples and rich eggplant hues lend to opening you up to your own intrinsic wealth and nobility.**

TOP RIGHT: **Ombre blues hint at the depths of wisdom that lead to insight, healing, and growth.**

BOTTOM LEFT: **Mirrors can invite us to see ourselves as we are, without obscuration.**

BOTTOM RIGHT: **The bedroom is your most sacred space, so make it a place that you can retreat to for rest and support.**

ABOVE: **Just like you, your bed doesn't have to be perfectly made all the time! Let it be lived in.**

The headboard

Ideally, you want your bed to have a headboard. From a feng shui perspective, a headboard offers you support. It also has a superpower: it can function as a support even when you are not in your bed sleeping. Your bed with its headboard is always there and it's always ready to receive you. You don't have to hold it all up on your own, you have help.

When you have this structure, it's like a strong back with a spine that holds you upright regardless of what happens. The headboard also connects the partners in the bed. Meaning that if you have a romantic bed partner, it connects the two of you. But if you are single, it can unify the yin and yang sides of you. In general, I'm talking about a solid and sturdy headboard that is securely fastened to the bed. If you have a choice, it's best to avoid headboards that are flimsy, have holes, bars, or similar. And the most important part is that it is connected physically to the bed.

As I always say, do the best you can with what you have. But in general, these are the guidelines. I have met many clients that simply refuse to have a headboard. And really, it's okay. It's your home, not mine. However, it's helpful to investigate the why behind that resistance, and see what you come up with. I've run into a strong and fierce pushback to this recommendation very often. I regard it as a prompt to invite the individual to dive deeper. There may be some gold down there at the bottom of the ocean.

Space for two

The size of the bed also matters. If you are an adult, and you want a healthy, balanced romantic relationship, it's best to have a bed that has space for two. Once a friend was Instagram-stalking (or as she says "researching") her crush, and we weren't completely sure if he was single until we saw a photograph of his bed. It was a twin mattress, up against a wall, with one pillow, and a cute dog on it. This is a dead giveaway: he's single. And later she remarked that, upon reflection, he probably wasn't ready to be in a relationship.

What I'm getting at here is, if you are sleeping in a twin or single sized bed, and would like a partner in your life, it's time to get a larger bed. If you have a single bed, there's literally no room to accommodate another person into this most private part of your life. You're not making space for your future partner. Or maybe you're just not in the place where you want a partner, and that's acceptable, too.

This is also true if you have a larger bed with room for two but somehow there is one lonely pillow, and one side of the bed is pushed up against the wall. I don't know about you, but I want my own pillow (or two) and certainly don't want to be the one sleeping trapped next to the wall.

It is also helpful to look at your space for two in regard to the nightstands. Do you have a nightstand on each side of the bed? It's helpful to have enough space and a nightstand for each partner's (or future partner's) side of the bed. It's also applicable in balancing your yin and yang. It always feels good to be welcomed and accommodated. And we all want a place to set our glass of water, and a spot to call our own. Again, this is true for each partner, but also the yin and yang aspects of your own self. The nightstands don't need to be perfectly symmetrical carbon copies of each other, but think instead how they can complement one another.

Clear the qi

When it comes to beds, but especially mattresses, be aware of the qi. Does it hold the vibration of an ex-partner, or energy that you may be ready to let go of? This is especially true after a transition. Be sure to clear the qi and set a new intention for the mattress and bed.

Also look at what's underneath your bed. We spend many unconscious hours sleeping in our bed, so of course the qi of what we sleep over affects us. If you must store things under your bed, stick to sleep-related items such as linens, pillows, and blankets. Definitely steer away from emotionally charged objects such as weapons, memorabilia from past partners, and even shoes can be too active. Find another place for those items in the home.

Bed linens

With regard to the bed linens, it's easy to overlook our pajamas, sheets, linens, blankets, and pillows. The materials, including textiles, that we surround ourselves with while we are sleeping affect us. Our skin is our largest organ and we can absorb qi very easily when we are asleep. We can make more conscious decisions in our choices that include examining the life energy interwoven in those fabrics. We can also make active decisions to purchase the best that we can afford. Consider if they are natural organic fibers, what is the lifecycle of the materials, how long do they take to biodegrade? How is it produced, and is it non-toxic next to your body while you sleep? What is the life experience of the hands, the people—all sentient beings—that created these materials. And of course, do the best you can. (As a sidenote: you can also find local animal shelters to which you can donate your threadbare linens; they typically need them.)

Minimize electronics

In our electronic device-driven world, take heed of the gadgets around you when you sleep. If your sleep is compromised, try minimizing the use of devices after sunset. Regardless of your sleep, if you recognize that you need time to slow down, also consider removing devices from the bedroom. This can be part of how you do your unscheduled day mindful ritual from Chapter 4.

The feeling-tone of your bedroom

Finally, take some time to see and feel the tone of your bedroom. Look at the colors as well as the imagery that you perceive in this space.

When you look at the artwork, check and see if the imagery and colors are consistent with what your bedroom symbolizes. Is it restful, is it healing? You may have read somewhere that it's "good feng shui" to have a pair of everything in the bedroom. This might be helpful for you, especially if you are ready to invite in a new partner, or continue to grow with your current relationship. But sometimes it's totally appropriate to have strong and solitary imagery if you're in a place where you want to heal your own heart.

Five element bedroom color guide

Color-wise, check in and see if the colors in your bedroom reflect the energies you want, need, or require. You can use the five elements to guide your color selections of paint, accessories, furniture, linens, artwork, and basically anything in the bedroom.

- Yellows, browns, earthy tones are **Earth** element colors that are cozy, stable, and grounding. But they can also keep you hibernating if you're prone to hiding in your cave
- Whites, off-whites, grays, metallics are **Metal** element colors that are crisp and clear. But sometimes they can be too sharp, so adding in other colors with white will be helpful if you need some softness and nurturing
- Blacks, charcoals, midnight blues are **Water** element colors that can offer elegance, depth, and deepening. But they are not the most uplifting if you're prone to depression or actually working through great sadness
- Blues, greens, teals are **Wood** element colors that heal, uplift, and can energize. But if you want more rest and support, the brighter tones might provide too much energy
- Reds and intense oranges are **Fire** element colors that inspire and create passion. Use red selectively—a little goes a long way. It might be hard to sleep if you have too much fire in your bedroom

ABOVE: **Any of the five elements can come into the bedroom with simple accessories like pillows. You can shift them with the seasons or based on what energies you require at any given time.**

Activate the tai qi of your bedroom

I would like to close this chapter with a very simple and direct way to work with the qi of the bedroom. Activate and bring light, curiosity, and transformative energy into your life by hanging a single feng shui crystal ball from the ceiling in the center of your bedroom using a red ribbon. Offer the intention of bringing clarity, light, and openness to any gifts the universe has to offer you.

nourish yourself: the kitchen

- The stove: your wealth and resources
- Feng shui shifts for your kitchen
- The energetics of food
  - Five element food color guide
  - Mindful eating
  - Mantra water

The kitchen is a space dedicated to supporting your body, family, and home. In feng shui, the kitchen embodies Earth element energy, which includes nourishment, health, and resources, as well as the element of Fire, which include the qualities of vitality and transformation. The kitchen is where you store and create the food that offers sustenance, qi, and nourishment to your body and spirit.

the stove: your wealth and resources

In feng shui, our kitchen, and especially the stove, affects our health, wealth, resources, and overall well-being. This is because how well we can feed ourselves directly affects how well we can thrive in the world. We need healthy minds and bodies. The function of a kitchen is to cook food for eating; therefore the qi of the kitchen greatly affects the energetics of our meals. In many modern open plan kitchens, the stove is the hearth: it's where we gather to connect with our families and loved ones. It's the heart of our home.

Commanding position of the stove

The stove is one of the three most important areas in your home, while the other two are the bed and the desk. It's essential to review the commanding position of your stove and burners (or hotplates). When you are cooking food on your stove, it is alchemy. You are changing and transforming the meal with the Fire element, and your qi. The quality and state of your qi while you cook directly affects your food, and therefore your health and well-being. And yes, this is even true if you don't cook very much. The qi is still connected to the stove.

You learned all about the commanding position in Chapter 2, but there are some specifics when it comes to the stove. We want to eat food that is created with relaxed and smooth qi. But when we are not in command while cooking at our stove, we may be infusing our meals with a subtle level of anxiety and fear. When you are standing at your stove cooking, you ideally want to be able to see all of the major doorways to the room, without your back facing any of them. To be in a commanding position, you want to be able to see all the doorways clearly, so you're not surprised while cooking. If you are not in the commanding position at your stove, don't worry. Keep reading!

OPPOSITE: **If you have a stove in the center (tai qi position) of your home, it may burn up your resources. It's helpful to add some Water element with black, as well as Earth element with browns and yellows to cool down the Fire element.**

Many times, it's not possible to reposition a stove that is out of command because it's not a piece of furniture that you can easily relocate. In this case, it's completely acceptable to correct your view and perspective with a mirror. The simplest solution is a strategically placed 3in (8cm) round convex mirror so that when you are standing and cooking at the burners, you can easily see any and all door openings. Be mindful that it's not too close to any heat source that can cause damage. And keep it clean!

Activate the qi of your stove

After you have confirmed you are in the commanding position, it's helpful to look at a few more feng shui aspects of your stove.

- Use your stove daily. It's important to keep the Fire energy stoked, and don't let that fire burn out. Use it daily, even if just to boil water for tea
- Keep it clean and tidy. Your stove and burners cannot breathe if they are covered with grease or food debris
- Make sure all the burners are functioning. If there is a part of your stove or a burner that needs repair, get it taken care of. Otherwise it may impart the same kind of stagnant qi into your home, health, and resources
- Double your burners, double your wealth. When you have more burners in the kitchen, there is more qi available. You can use a mirror to reflect the burners, and so double them energetically. In fact, the mirror you use to correct your commanding position can do extra duty here if it also reflects your burners. Another easy way to double the energy of the burners is to securely attach a flat 3in (8cm) round mirror facing down so it reflects the burners below it. This can be fastened to the ceiling or to the bottom side of your stove vent (hood). Be sure that the mirror is kept clean and safe from heat

Mindful stove ritual

Do you have a favorite burner on your stove? Currently, mine is the one in the front to the right.

There are so many ways that we become accustomed to the qi in our homes. I see this often with the stove, which affects our wealth, resources, and health. Without much thought, we tend to beeline toward the same burner every time. And in this way, our habitual patterns begin to become deeply ingrained in the qi of our home. In life we often easily glide along these habitually walked paths. However, if we simply change our view, we may be able to perceive different threads of opportunity. Or just an interesting new detail.

ABOVE: **Keep your kitchen and stove clean for the best feng shui. Fresh greenery also nourishes us with Wood element.**

Tomorrow morning when you go to use your stove, see if you can catch yourself before you go on autopilot and turn on a burner without intention. I invite you to take a mindful moment for a stove ritual to thoughtfully choose the burner you will light up. It's totally okay if it's the same one that you always use, because you've made an intentional choice. It's about the pause, and your awareness. This is also recommended as a daily morning ritual. It only takes a few moments. Look and see what happens in your life, as you begin to purposely make small shifts toward more awareness. Through subtle moves, we can start slowly to unravel our habitual patterns with gentle kindness.

feng shui shifts for your kitchen

Here are some important aspects to review when it comes to your kitchen's feng shui.

Chipped and broken items

If you have chipped or broken dishes or homewares, it's helpful to remove them from the kitchen as eating implements. They can be useful in other rooms as functional items (like using a treasured yet chipped mug as your pencil holder). They can also be upcycled into art, or you can explore other creative options.

The Japanese practice of kintsugi ("golden joinery") is also a consideration. The idea is to repair a broken or chipped item so that it is not only usable but transforms it into an even more precious object. Traditionally, kintsugi uses gold to make the repair, but you can research other ways to repair that are inspired by the kintsugi process.

Clear the qi

We cook and store our food in the kitchen area. As with clutter in the other parts of the home, it's helpful to pay attention to the qi of your refrigerator and pantry. The qi of food that is unwanted, expired, infested with pests, and/or stale will affect your energy. Regularly clear and clean out these areas. Use non-toxic natural cleaning products. Compost, or dispose of excess food as best you can. You can also regularly employ any of my recommended space clearing methods in conjunction with your cleaning. It's especially powerful to deep-clean the kitchen on the spring and autumnal equinoxes, and the winter and summer solstices, since these seasonal calendar events also correspond to a shift in the qi of the food that we consume.

Compost your food scraps

Joy comes from recognizing our interdependence with the world. This includes acknowledging what we leave behind. You can start by caring where your food scraps go. Instead of tossing them into the rubbish bin, you can compost. I live in New York City, where we are fortunate to have municipal compost drop off locations with their own specific guidelines on what can be composted. Research your area and explore what is appropriate for you with the energy and space that you have available.

Healing herbs

The plant kingdom offers many remarkable healing botanicals. Even the ordinary spices and herbs in our pantry can offer gifts. They can be infused into teas, eaten with our meals, and many can be burnt and offered in botanical smoke blessings (see Chapter 5). You can grow herbs, work with them fresh or dried, or as essential oils, drink herbal teas, or simply have them in your spice drawer. It's also fun to explore the healing medicinal herbs and plants that are local to your area, as well as connected to your personal cultural heritage.

My current favorites are ginger to ground me and support my digestion. The other is stinging nettles in the spring, to remind me it's okay to be prickly sometimes. If any of this sparks some interest, here's your invitation to explore healing herbs. If you have or start your own kitchen garden, it has the added bonus of bringing in the Wood element.

Activate the qi of your kitchen

Clear quartz is a mineral crystal that can enhance qi, especially if it's programmed with your intention. Place your quartz in fresh water under moonlight for one night. The next day, hold the crystal in both hands and impart the intention that this clear quartz will invite the deity of your kitchen to amplify the healing life force energy of the food you eat. Then with a humble heart, place the clear quartz into your refrigerator. Please dispose of the water from this ceremony by taking it outside and offering it to the earth nearby.

ABOVE: **Growing your favorite herbs in the kitchen is a wonderful way to balance the Wood element.**

the energetics of food

Food sustains our qi. But it also cultivates culture, connection, and pleasure. Just like in our bodies and our homes, life energy breathes within our food. But just as humanity has lost its connection to nature, there's also a modern disconnect between qi, food, health, and our bodies.

Food is medicine. It deeply saddens me when we avert our eyes from our modern food systems. It's so easy to look at an anonymous block of food and have no idea or care as to where it comes from or its life story. What was the environment like, the land, the weather; where did this food come from? What was the life experience of the water in your glass, or the egg in your refrigerator? What about the humans that grew, collected, or cooked the food?

We can reflect and be curious about all of it. Explore the qi that created the food. Our food affects us. The qi of our food vibrates with the energy of those that took part in its way to our dinner plates. I believe we have a responsibility to look deeper for the sake of our own health, that of our families, and the entire planet. At the very least, I invite you to use your wealth and resources to obtain the highest quality, ethically produced food, and see how it circles back to support you.

LEFT: **Using generous bowls with a wide mouth encourages sharing and community.**

RIGHT: **A variety of colors in the kitchen brings health, as does including a rainbow of hues on your dinner plate. Explore the color energetics with the decor of your kitchen.**

Five Element Food Color Guide

We can apply five element theory to our food as well. We can look at the color and other characteristics of foods to see how they may connect to one or more of the elements. You can work with the foods that offer you the elements you need or that support the season you are in. Note: If this is interesting to you, also be sure to check out nutrition and food teachings from Chinese medicine. This is only a brief and general application from a color perspective.

Earth element:

Yellow, brown, and earthy colors. The taste of earth is sweet. Root vegetables, whole grains, and sweet fruits are the Earth element.

Metal element:

White, off-white, and gray colors. The taste of metal is spicy. Onions, cauliflower, apples, and other white foods are the Metal element.

ABOVE: **A bowl of fresh fruit creates qi of abundance, prosperity, and fruition.**

Water element:

Black, charcoal, and midnight blue colors. The taste of water is salty. Fresh water, black beans, black rice, kidney beans, and other dark purple or black foods are the Water element.

Wood element:

Blue, green, and teal colors. The taste of wood is sour. Vibrant greens, plants, sprouts, and sour fruits are the Wood element.

Fire element:

Red and fiery orange colors. The taste of fire is bitter. Bitter dark greens, tomatoes, strawberries and other red and/or heart-shaped foods are the Fire element.

OPPOSITE: **Creating moments for meals with flowers, a placemat, and care go a long way to promote the health and vitality of a home, even if it's just for one or two people.**

Mindful eating ritual

This is a mindful eating ritual that is an experiential practice and reminder to become more aware of your food.

- Find a quiet place to be alone. Remove all distractions
- Set your timer for nine minutes
- Eat one piece of food of your choice. I recommend an apple, but you could also do this with a single raisin or small piece of dark chocolate
- Use the full nine minutes to slowly eat your apple
- No talking, no devices, just you and the apple

Mantra water

Water is so vital for our well-being and feng shui acknowledges this. If you recall, feng shui means "wind" and "water"—the water that we drink flows through our bodies, and is our elixir of life. Creating your own mantra water is one way you can imbue water with intention and healing qi for yourself, and in harmony with the planet, the sun, and the moon. In this ritual we use the Sanskrit mantra Om ma ni pad me hum, which roughly translates to "the jewel is in the lotus."

Guidelines for creating mantra water:

- Fill your container with the freshest and cleanest drinking water available
- Chant the mantra "*Om ma ni pad me hum*" into the water 108 times. Allow the vibrations of your voice to resonate with the water
- Allow the vessel to sit under the light of the moon and the sun for one night/day cycle
- Decant into another container or pour directly into your drinking glass

You can drink this water, or offer it to your shrine. You can also get fancy and add non-water soluble and non-toxic crystals like clear or rose quartz, amethyst, or citrine. I suggest you find a beautiful glass container that you love. Please dedicate this vessel, keep it sacred, and use it only for creating mantra water.

OPPOSITE: **Water gifts us life qi. Allow it to flow, heal, and revitalize you.**

align with your path in life: your workspace

Although this chapter is about your workspace, I am actually referring to the area of your home that is connected to your *raison d'être*. *Raison d'être* is a French expression that means your reason for being. What is your motivation and path in this life? And how can you offer your gifts to the world?

When I started my spiritual journey, it didn't take me very long to wonder how I could integrate more meaning, inspiration, joy, and satisfaction into my career as an architect. We spend a tremendous amount of our waking hours invested in our work. Please keep in mind that my definition of career is inclusive of many types of work: stay at home parent, aspiring fine artist, company worker, entrepreneur, retired, volunteer, forever student, or if you don't have a formal "job" at all.

I know that this topic can be a bit challenging or button-pushing, because not everyone is satisfied with their "career" or "job." Perhaps you have not yet uncovered what your path in life is. But I invite you to step back and see how this can apply to whatever your situation is. Be creative, inclusive, and curious. Also, please be kind and gentle with yourself. Remember to do the best you can with what you have. Your unique career situation is included in what follows, however it is expressed in your life at this moment.

the desk: your path in life

Feng shui wise, we've already looked at the other two important areas in your home: the bed and the stove. The third home area is the desk because it represents your career and path in life, your expression in the world. What is your reason for being, and how can you appreciate your own gifts?

In this chapter, I'll refer to a formal desk. It's always best to have your own desk at home. However, these suggestions are also applicable to a temporary desk area like your set up at the dining room or coffee table, a workspace at an outside office, a co-working space, or even the table you've scoped out at the coffee shop. With your open mind, this chapter accommodates most variations on where you set up your desk.

OPPOSITE: **Living green plants in a brown pot can bring stability as well as kindness and flexibility into your home and work life.**

Dedicate a space just for you

Your desk is a space that is dedicated just for you. It's your spot to focus on your path in life and reason for being. If you don't have one already, look as to how you can create a little place for yourself somewhere in your home. Make space to cultivate joy and inspiration. Sometimes this means a space for your art, or your hobbies, your writing, or even so you can answer your emails with ease.

If you don't have a formal desk, you can create a miniature desk area with a desk blotter. A desk blotter is a flat rectangular material with some weight that you can roll out and use as a workspace. It protects the surface below, and also offers you some stability and support. It can act energetically like a mini desk. (See more about this below in the "stability" section, page 128.)

Dedicate a place that allows you room to cultivate your gifts to the world. This is the space meant just for you, so that you can focus on what inspires you, your *raison d'être*. Take a moment to acknowledge and offer gratitude to this space that you have carved out for yourself. Say hello and thank you to your desk.

Commanding position of the desk

The commanding position is also very important when it comes to your workspace. This translates to being able to see clearly in your work and career. You can be more relaxed and not worried about surprises. Instead, when in the commanding position you can see all the opportunities coming your way. You are moving forward with your eyes open and with full awareness, preparation, and ease.

When you are sitting at your desk, you want to be able to see the door while not being directly in line with it. Like with the bed, the easiest way to achieve this is to have your desk situated in a diagonal from the door. However, it's a little challenging with the desk, because not everyone has lots of space in their home. Whatever your desk position is, do your best to set yourself up so you can see the door and not be directly aligned with it. If that's not possible, a mirror can be used to correct this. For the desk, a small convex mirror placed around your computer screen works very well to offer a wider view all around. Just make sure you can see the door in that mirror. If you have to sit right in front of a door, you can use the feng shui crystal ball to disperse any qi. Hang it from the ceiling with a red string, somewhere between your desk and the door. You can refer to Chapter 2 for more details on the commanding position and the crystal ball.

Examples of the commanding position for a desk.

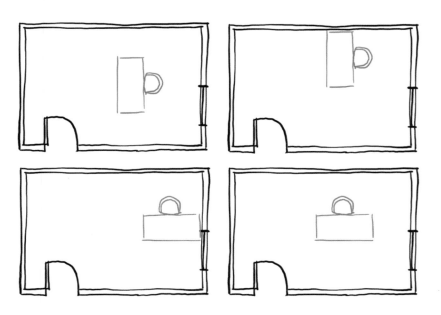

Activate the bagua mandala of your desk

The feng shui bagua mandala can also be overlaid on your desk. If your desk is rectangular, you can lay the bagua aligned with the bottom of the desk which is where you sit. If you have an L-shaped desk, it's similar to a rectangle. You can align the bottom of the bagua where you sit at the primary part of the desk, and you can disregard the side.

If you have an odd-shaped desk, or one that moves around (like your kitchen island that later becomes your breakfast bar), you can also use a desk blotter (mentioned earlier) that is rectangular to act as your desk mandala. If you're working with a small desk, or with the desk blotter, you can use one of the corresponding crystals from the crystal bagua mandala in lieu of these larger objects for activation (see Chapter 3). Be sure to infuse the crystal with the intention connected to the gua.

Once you figure out the bagua mandala on your desk, you can see if there are any areas that you want to work with. I would limit the bagua activations to three areas at a time. Keep it simple!

Zhen: New Beginnings, Family

If you need a kick start in beginning projects or anything new, you can work this area of your desk. You can record the name and details of the project on a sheet of paper, place it in a red envelope, and place it in the Zhen area of your desk.

Xun: Abundance, Prosperity, Wealth

A living green plant in a black pot, or your mantra water container (see Chapter 7) may be located in the wealth corner of your desk with the intention to provide steady and expansive growth in your career.

Tai Qi: Health, Overall Well-being, Center

Since this is the center of the desk, it's hard to place anything here. But if you need general and overall support in your work life, use a desk blotter. The flat, square-ish shape will offer grounding and stability.

LEFT: **Red envelopes are special in feng shui. They represent auspicious intention, protection, celebration and vibrant life energy.**

OPPOSITE: **Your desktop gives you the space to mindfully curate your path in life. What area will you activate today?**

Qian: Benefactors, Helpful People, Travel

This area can attract helpful people as well as benefactors in your life. If you need some of this qi, you can ring a bell in this corner of your desk to call in any help you need.

Dui: Completion, Children, Joy

If you need some extra qi to complete projects, you can write the name and details on a sheet of paper placed in a red envelope. You can locate this in the Dui position of your desk.

Gen: Knowledge, Self-Cultivation, Skills

Sometimes we need to learn and cultivate more skills in order to move forward. Try placing a heavy paperweight in this area to give you the encouragement to increase your knowledge.

Li: Recognition, Fame, Visibility

If you need more visibility or more inspiration, this can be the gua for you. Place a living green plant here to feed the Fire element, so you have the resources and qi to shine in the sun.

Kan: Path in Life, Career, Wisdom

When you are at your desk, you are probably sitting in Kan position. When you bestow time, space, and attention on your desk, you activate the qi of your path in life, your career, and your wisdom.

Kun: Relationships, Partners, Self-Love

It's helpful to be open to receiving when it comes to work. You can find an open bowl or other container, one that is precious to you, and place this in the relationship corner so that you are open to receiving. It should have a wide mouth, and not be easy to tip over.

TOP LEFT: **A metal bell vibrates your voice, while red brings good luck and inspiration.**

TOP RIGHT: **Glass can bring clarity, and the weight of a heavy object offers stability.**

BOTTOM LEFT: **Fresh (especially fragrant) flowers can unstick the energy when you find yourself stuck.**

BOTTOM RIGHT: **In general, soft and rounded leaves resonate soft, gentle, flowing qi.**

feng shui shifts for your workspace

Here are some other considerations when looking at the feng shui of your workspace.

What is your view?

Take a moment to observe your view from your desk. Are you looking at a wall or through a window? Are you staring at your bed or your refrigerator? What you see while you are sitting at your desk affects your qi. What is your view? If you feel any resistance or "yes, but..." comes up, I encourage you to take note of it. Remember, this is your home and you can decide what it is that is most important to implement.

If you are looking at a wall very close to you (within 27in (68cm), or within arm's length). This may affect your ability to progress and see ahead in your career. It's like you're staring at, and being stopped, by a brick wall. The best way to correct this is to mirror the wall. An easy way to implement this is to get a full-length mirror and hang it horizontally behind your desk.

If you are set up to gaze out your window, especially onto a lovely view, this is not the best feng shui for your desk. Your qi flows right out out the window rather than staying with the task at hand. It's better to rearrange your desk so that you can turn to the side and enjoy the view when you take short breaks. I don't know about you, but I prefer to be focused while at my desk, and then when that work is done, walk outside and be in the view rather than peer at it from my desk all day.

What you look at while sitting at your desk affects you. If you are looking at your bed from your desk, it might feel ever so much easier to nap rather than finish that important deadline. Or if you're set up so that you are looking at the kitchen, you might find yourself thinking about snacks or get distracted planning out your next meal. In general, it's better to set up your desk so that you can clearly see the door (without being directly in front of it), so you are in command with the widest view of the room.

Do you have enough room?

Do you have enough space for your desk? Is the desk big enough for what you need, and would you benefit from more generosity in this respect? Next, look at the space around the desk and where you sit. At the bare minimum, there should be at least 36in (91cm) for your chair to move

ABOVE: **Take care to allow space to grow, explore, and to expand in front and behind your desk. Do the best with what you have.**

around. If you feel squeezed in and have a challenge walking to and from your desk area, this also creates obstacles and difficulties in how your qi flows, and how qi can find you.

Lift your qi and focus

We have so many distractions in our modern lives, including the notification pop-ups of emails, texts, calendar events, let alone the myriad tasks and complexities we encounter. In feng shui, mirrors serve many magical functions. This is a subtle and intentional feng shui adjustment that you can use to improve your focus and uplift your qi while sitting at your desk.

At noon, on any given day, mindfully clean a brand new, flat, 3in (7cm) diameter, clear glass mirror. Polish it gently with the intention that it's a feng shui talisman that will lift your energy and focus your qi. Then securely fasten it to the ceiling above where you sit at your desk. The mirror side shall face down and align with the crown of your head. Keep it there indefinitely, and be sure to keep it clean, dust free, and fastened without any worry of it falling.

RIGHT: **Create a workspace with room to inspire, play, and allow for a little bit of chaos.**

Earth element for stability

If you'd like to bring in overall grounding, stability, and security in your career and work, bring in the earth element with a desk blotter. A desk blotter is a sturdy material that is rectangular and flat. You can keep this on your desk, or you can roll it out daily to create your energetic desk of support wherever you're working.

When you select a color, I would first recommend you select the color you are attracted to. It's helpful to then look at the color you selected based on the five element color guide below. If you are at a loss as to what color to choose, then alternatively, you can look to the five elements to guide your decision.

Desk blotter five element color guide

Earth element for balance, grounding, and support
Colors: Yellows, browns, earthy tones
Metal element for joy, productivity, and completion
Color: Whites, off-whites, grays, metallics
Water element for wisdom, connections, and intuition
Color: Blacks, charcoals, midnight blues
Wood element for expansion, growth, and starting something new
Color: Blues, greens, teals
Fire element for visibility, improved reputation, and inspiration
Color: Reds and fiery oranges

Energetic desk boundaries

The Earth element is also about boundaries. I've noticed that this is something we are all working with, how to balance work and life, and to explore our energetic boundaries. In addition, in the digital age it's also helpful to acknowledge and consider our boundaries in light of video conference meetings. For the first time, many of us may be opening our homes to the energy of others through video calls. There is value in considering what boundaries are important for you and how to implement them. This includes time, space, and energy.

One way to acknowledge and assume responsibility for how energy may or may not enter your home via a computer is to look at your desk. One feng shui adjustment can be to create an energetic crystal grid at your desk, with the intention to filter the qi around your work, desk, and possible video conferences. You can create a desk grid by placing a black crystal in each of the four corners of your desk. I recommend black tourmaline or

ABOVE: **A variety of textures and seating options can offer creative opportunities. How can you see diverse perspectives with fresh eyes?**

black obsidian. You can have the crystals sit on top of your desk, in drawers, or even have them securely fastened under the desktop. Be sure to visualize the intention of protection, so that any unknown qi must first ask for permission and only with your consent expand beyond the grid you've created.

interconnecting home and community

- We are interconnected with our spaces
- Opening doors to compassion
- Deepen your community with the dining table
- One flower in a vase offering
- *Ichi-go ichi-e*

we are interconnected with our spaces

The number nine is the most auspicious number in feng shui and represents completion. Similarly, this last chapter completes the wheel and reminds us to circle back to the connection between mindfulness and feng shui. The mindful practice of feng shui can go much deeper than looking at our own personal needs. Let's begin to look at how we can step out and connect to our communities with joy, generosity, and friendliness.

opening doors to compassion

Feng shui sees doors as portals for qi, allowing energy to come in and out of your home. Doors also represent your voice and communication. Your home's formal front door is what we call in feng shui "the mouth of qi"—the main gateway to receive qi into your home and life. Compassion is a practice that is not just about giving but receiving. Be curious and notice what changes occur when you implement the front door feng shui suggestions.

OPPOSITE: Inspired by a Jewish prayer:
May the door of this home be wide enough to receive love and fellowship.
May the door of this home be narrow enough to keep us safe and protected.

Activate your mouth of qi

It's helpful to activate your front door, so you can invite fresh qi into your home, and also begin to connect to the outside world in a new way. I am referring to your formal front door, which may not be the same door that is used most often to move in and out of your home.

- Use your front door at least once a day, even simply to collect the mail
- Regularly clean the door surface itself, as well as the frame, the threshold, the doormat, hinges, and handles. Oil any squeaks and make sure everything is functioning properly
- Allow the door to open a full 90° if possible. Allow your connection to the world to be as free and clear as it can be. If there is clutter or furniture blocking the doorway, find a new place for it
- Take a moment to walk the path a guest would walk through your entrance. First, walk out of your home through the front door and to the street. Then take the same path back. Notice if there are any obstacles that can be removed, and make sure that your front door is easy to identify and clearly labeled with the house number
- Offer fresh flowers in the entry area (outside or inside) as often as you can (see below for the "One flower in a Vase" suggestion)

One good deed a day

This was the very first feng shui adjustment that my mentor offered me. This feng shui adjustment taught me the importance of doors. My good deed revealed itself as literally opening doors for others. But what I received from this teaching was that by opening doors to others, I was opening doors for myself. Please do not let my experience flavor yours. I'll be curious to see what opens up for you.

- For 27 days, perform one good deed a day
- If you miss a day, start all over again

There are no guidelines for the good deed.

TOP LEFT: **Fierce compassion.** What are your personal symbols of protection that can be positioned at your mouth of qi?

TOP RIGHT: **A space for qi to gather at the entry helps to create a smooth transition. An inbetween, from inside to outside, yin to yang.**

BOTTOM LEFT: **While everything doesn't need to be matchy-matchy, there is a simple honesty in symmetry. Things can be the same while also being different.**

BOTTOM RIGHT: **There are opportunities to hold the door open—to invite. What is it that you'd like to formally invite into your life?**

deepen your community with the dining table

Over the past few years, I've been hearing consistently that clients and students are yearning for deeper friendships, connection with community, and a sense of belonging. The dining table is a symbol of community and friendship. It is where we feast, connect, relax, and enjoy conversation together.

Many homes no longer have a formal dining room, but feng shui still discovers value in any dining area you can make space for. If you're longing for community, take a look at what's happening in your dining area. This is one of our feng shui connections to the outside world.

Make space for company

In regards to size and seating, ideally you want your dining table as large as you can accommodate without being excessively large for the space. For instance, if you only have a tiny bistro table with one chair, there is only room for you. A larger table and more chairs invites more qi into your home. The more dining area seating you have, the more friendships you can hold.

Invite friends into your heart

Where your dining table is placed in the home also makes an energetic impact. If possible, locate the dining table further into your home. When the dining table is right next to the front door, it may mean that your friendships don't go very deep. You may not be opening your home or heart to a deeper connection. You do the best with what you have.

OPPOSITE: **Windows represent the eyes. Keep them clean and in good repair so that you can clearly see and experience your world.**

one flower in a vase offering

This is a simple and beautiful practice that you can do anytime you desire a connection to the world. This offering also creates a miniature world, an expression of the five elements, and invites in nature spirits wherever they are needed.

Earth element is your vase, which holds and provides stability.
Metal element is the cutters you use to trim the stem, clearing any obstacles in your path.
Water element is the fresh water you offer, the life blood of all sentient beings.
Wood element is the flower itself, bringing expansive and uplifting life and joy.
Fire element is the sunlight that created the flower: all living beings yearn, grow, and look toward the sun.

Guidelines:

- Step out your door and wander aimlessly toward a place where you may receive one single flower. This may include a visit to your garden, somewhere in nature, a flower shop, or even your local grocery store
- Invite the flower to find you. Look and see what is available, what has life and freshness. You can be curious and notice what flowers you are attracted to today
- Humbly ask the flower for permission to make it part of your one flower in a vase offering in your home. If you receive a yes, you may take the flower home. And yes, you may purchase a bunch of flowers, and use the other flowers elsewhere
- Locate the appropriate container for your flower and clean it well.
- Fill the chosen vessel with fresh water as you would for your honored guest to drink. Not too full that it will spill—slightly over half full
- Use your cutters to trim away at least an inch of the bottom stem, as a kindness to the flower, so it can drink
- Mindfully place your one single bloom in the vase, noticing the way in which it may or may not face the sun. And notice how it may change when the sun sets
- Generously offer clean fresh water daily, trim the stem as required
- When the flower begins to expire, notice when it is the best time to let it go
- When the flower has died, say goodbye with ceremony by gently cutting it into smaller pieces and wrapping it in biodegradable paper. You may then dispose of it appropriately

OPPOSITE: **One bloom. One chair. One moment. One of you. One thing at a time. Simplicity is the key.**

ichi-go ichi-e

Ichi-go ichi-e is a Japanese saying that I learned in tea ceremony class. It means "one time, one meeting" and reminds us to treasure each present moment. In tea class, we make the same cup of tea every time in the same way, however each experience is different. The same and also different. Things change even though it may seem like an ordinary everyday occurrence. We can notice and celebrate the subtle love notes from the phenomenal world. What is the humidity like right now? Does the tea taste stronger than it did yesterday? What does the water sound like when it's poured into a cold cup versus a warm cup? These precious details highlight the beauty in the world and within us.

We are in a relationship with everything around us. There are countless causes and conditions that brought us to this very moment. We can appreciate our lives and treasure the gift of humanity on this earth. When we become aware of our interdependence with the home and our outer environments, we can also begin to open our eyes and hearts to the interconnection that includes all sentient beings, including our earth.

I am grateful for our "one time, one meeting." I hope that this book has invited you to examine how we are interconnected with our homes, and offers you inspiration to create spaciousness and joy in your life. Your life and your home are seeds of potential; like an acorn from an oak tree, you contain all the wisdom and all the potential within you. You are the tree and the seed at the same time.

Om ma ni pad me hum

The jewel is within the lotus

OPPOSITE: **Honor all the different strands that create the beautiful container that is you. A basket open to hold and receive the gifts of this world.**

index

picture credits

All photography the copyright of Ryland Peters & Small/CICO Books:

1 ph. Polly Wreford; 2 ph. Polly Wreford; 3 ph. Rachel Whiting; 4–5 ph. Polly Wreford; 7 ph. Debi Treloar; 8 ph. Paul Massey; 9 ph. Rachel Whiting; 11 ph. Polly Wreford; 12 ph. Catherine Gratwicke; 14 ph. Catherine Gratwicke; 15 ph. Edina Van Der Wyck; 16–17 ph. Rachel Whiting; 18 ph. Polly Wreford; 19 ph. Polly Wreford; 20 above right ph. Debi Treloar; 20 centre ph. Simon Brown; 20 below right ph. Debbie Patterson; 21 above right ph. Rachel Whiting; 21 below left ph. Debi Treloar; 22 ph. Paul Massey; 23 ph. Debi Treloar; 25 ph. Paul Massey; 28 ph. Rachel Whiting; 30 ph. Paul Massey; 31 ph. Rachel Whiting; 32 ph. Rachel Whiting; 38 ph. Simon Brown; 39 ph. Paul Massey; 41 ph. Rachel Whiting; 42 above left ph. Emma Mitchell and Caroline Arber; 42 above right ph. Debi Treloar; 42 below left ph. Rachel Whiting; 42 below right ph. Paul Massey; 45 ph. Debi Treloar; 46 ph. Polly Wreford; 47 ph. Rachel Whiting; 48 ph. Polly Wreford; 49 ph. Rachel Whiting; 53 ph. Rachel Whiting; 55 ph. Debi Treloar; 58 ph. Emma Mitchell; 60 ph. Paul Ryan; 61 ph. Polly Wreford; 63 ph. Rachel Whiting; 64 ph. Emma Mitchell & Caroline Arber; 66 ph. Debi Treloar; 67 ph. Lisa Cohen; 68 ph. Christopher Drake; 71 ph. Catherine Gratwicke; 73 ph. Rachel Whiting; 74 ph. Rachel Whiting; 75 ph. Rachel Whiting; 77 ph. Rachel Whiting; 78 ph. Rachel Whiting; 81 ph. Debi Treloar; 82–83 ph. Paul Massey; 85 ph. Debi Treloar; 87 ph. Jan Baldwin; 88 ph. Polly Wreford; 89 ph. Paul Ryan; 91 ph. Rachel Whiting; 95 ph. Debi Treloar; 96 above left ph. Polly Wreford; 96 above right Penny Wincer and Gavin Kingcome; 96 below left ph. Polly Wreford; 96 below right ph. Polly Wreford; 98 ph. Polly Wreford; 100–101 ph. Debi Treloar; 102 ph. Simon Brown; 103 ph. Rachel Whiting; 105 ph. Catherine Gratwicke; 106–107 ph. Rachel Whiting; 108 above left ph. Rachel Whiting; 109 above right ph. Rachel Whiting; 110 left ph. Rachel Whiting; 110–111 ph. Rachel Whiting; 112 ph. Polly Wreford; 113 ph. Mark Lohman; 115 ph. Paul Massey; 116 ph. Polly Wreford; 117 ph. Polly Wreford; 119 ph. Rachel Whiting; 120 ph. Hans Blomquist; 122 ph. Penny Wincer; 123 ph. Catherine Gratwicke; 124 above left Ph. Lisa Cohen; 124 above right ph. Polly Wreford; 124 below left ph. Rachel Whiting; 124 below right ph. Rachel Whiting; 126 ph. Jan Baldwin; 127 ph. Rachel Whiting; 128–129 ph. Rachel Whiting; 130 ph. Catherine Gratwicke; 131 ph. Catherine Gratwicke; 133 ph. Jan Baldwin; 134 above left ph. Simon Brown; 134 above right ph. Catherine Gratwicke; 134 below left ph. Jan Baldwin; 134 below right ph. Lisa Cohen; 137 ph. Rachel Whiting; 138 ph. Paul Massey; 141 ph. Debi Treloar.

acknowledgments

It's a windy and rainy autumn day in France, day five of a meditation retreat. As I wandered through a small grove of oak trees this morning, I appreciated the cascading elder branches, heavy with wisdom. Their weathered leaves touched the earth. Then, a single verdant green acorn found its way to me.

The generosity of the tree begins in the spring as she creates an abundance of flowers that later form the fruit. When autumn arrives, the nourished acorns begin to fall away, ripe with nourishment.

Thank you to all my teachers. Each of you have generously given me true love, acceptance, kindness, enrichment, and space for me to find my voice. Each one of you has been a catalyst for creating an environment for my heart to open, be vulnerable, and find joy. Each one of you has offered me friendship as well as connecting me to my cultural heritage.

Through the vehicles of feng shui, flowers, art, and meditation, your dharma teachings introduced me to a language that I could understand. With this unspoken communication through qi, I found true, overflowing abundance. My thanks to each one of you for illuminating a life path I never could have imagined possible. You have offered patience and skillful guidance so that I may begin to awaken to this magical, beautiful, and precious world that we live in together. Thank you for your brilliance, and for being my mentor and spiritual friend.

Thank you to all of my teachers:

My *kalyāṇa-mittatā*, my dharma teacher: Marcia Shibata.

My feng shui teachers: Rosalie Prinzivalli, Katherine Metz, Steven Post, and Barry Gordon.

I am especially grateful to Katherine for writing the foreword, and both Katherine and Rosalie for being present while I was writing this book.

My root teachers: Vidyadhara Chögyam Trungpa Rinpoche and His Holiness Grandmaster Professor Lin Yun.

A special thanks to my work-wife, my co-conspirator at Mindful Design Feng Shui School: Laura Morris. Thank you for never asking anything of me and instead always walking by my side with support, for your strength and wisdom, and especially for giving me space and courage to embody both yin and yang.

I would also like to thank my friends that encouraged me as I wrote this book. They listened, cheered me on, and permitted me space to procrastinate: Nancy Guberti, Amy T. Won, and Tamsin Lee.

Thank you to my meditation instructors, past and present: especially Michele Laporte and David Nichtern.

This book would not have been possible without the support and persistence of my literary agent and dharma friend, William Clark, as well as my editors at CICO, Kristine Pidkameny and Slav Todorov.

And most importantly, thank you to my family, for always loving me and allowing me space to fall apart: Jeremiah Cymerman, Javier and Pearlita.

resources

To learn more and dive deeper, you can study or work with Anjie.

Listen to the Holistic Spaces Podcast
visit **anjiecho.com**

Study at Mindful Design Feng Shui School
visit **mindfuldesignschool.com**

Shop for curated feng shui items at the Holistic Spaces store
visit **holisticspaces.com**